W9-CDN-838

SOPHIE DE GROUCHY'S *LETTERS ON SYMPATHY*

OXFORD NEW HISTORIES OF PHILOSOPHY

Series Editors

Christia Mercer, Melvin Rogers, and Eileen O'Neill (1953–2017)

*

Advisory Board

Lawrie Balfour, Jacqueline Broad, Marguerite Deslauriers, Karen Detlefsen, Bachir Diagne, Don Garrett, Robert Gooding-Williams, Andrew Janiak, Marcy Lascano, Lisa Shapiro, Tommie Shelby

*

Oxford New Histories of Philosophy provides essential resources for those aiming to diversify the content of their philosophy courses, revisit traditional narratives about the history of philosophy, or better understand the richness of philosophy's past. Examining previously neglected or understudied philosophical figures, movements, and traditions, the series includes both innovative new scholarship and new primary sources.

*

Published in the series

Mexican Philosophy in the 20ᵗʰ Century: Essential Readings
Edited by Carlos Alberto Sánchez and Robert Eli Sanchez, Jr.

Sophie de Grouchy's Letters on Sympathy: *A Critical Engagement with Adam Smith's* The Theory of Moral Sentiments
Translated by Sandrine Bergès. Edited by Sandrine Bergès and Eric Schliesser

Women Philosophers of Seventeenth-Century England: Selected Correspondence
Edited by Jacqueline Broad

SOPHIE DE GROUCHY'S
LETTERS ON SYMPATHY

A Critical Engagement with Adam Smith's *The Theory of Moral Sentiments*

Translated by Sandrine Bergès

WITH AN INTRODUCTION, GLOSSARY, AND COMMENTARY
BY SANDRINE BERGÈS AND ERIC SCHLIESSER

OXFORD
UNIVERSITY PRESS

OXFORD
UNIVERSITY PRESS

Oxford University Press is a department of the University of Oxford. It furthers
the University's objective of excellence in research, scholarship, and education
by publishing worldwide. Oxford is a registered trade mark of Oxford University
Press in the UK and certain other countries.

Published in the United States of America by Oxford University Press
198 Madison Avenue, New York, NY 10016, United States of America.

© Oxford University Press 2019

All rights reserved. No part of this publication may be reproduced, stored in
a retrieval system, or transmitted, in any form or by any means, without the
prior permission in writing of Oxford University Press, or as expressly permitted
by law, by license, or under terms agreed with the appropriate reproduction
rights organization. Inquiries concerning reproduction outside the scope of the
above should be sent to the Rights Department, Oxford University Press, at the
address above.

You must not circulate this work in any other form
and you must impose this same condition on any acquirer.

Library of Congress Cataloging-in-Publication Data
Names: Condorcet, Marie-Louise-Sophie de Grouchy, marquise de, 1764–1822,
author. | Bergès, Sandrine, editor, translator. | Schliesser, Eric, 1971–
editor, translator. | Container of (expression): Condorcet,
Marie-Louise-Sophie de Grouchy, marquise de, 1764–1822. Lettres sur la
sympathie. English (Bergès and Schliesser) | Container of (expression):
Condorcet, Marie-Louise-Sophie de Grouchy, marquise de, 1764–1822. Lettres
sur la sympathie. French (Bergès and Schliesser)
Title: Sophie de Grouchy's letters on sympathy / edited [and translated] by
Sandrine Bergès and Eric Schliesser.
Description: New York, NY, United States of America : Oxford University
Press, [2020] | Includes bibliographical references and index.
Identifiers: LCCN 2018038479 (print) | LCCN 2018040294 (ebook) |
ISBN 9780190637125 (online content) | ISBN 9780190637101 (updf) |
ISBN 9780190637118 (epub) | ISBN 9780190637095 (pbk. :alk. paper) |
ISBN 9780190637088 (cloth :alk. paper)
Subjects: LCSH: Condorcet, Marie-Louise-Sophie de Grouchy, marquise de,
1764–1822—Correspondence. | Condorcet, Jean-Antoine-Nicolas de Caritat,
marquis de, 1743–1794. | Statesmen's spouses—France—Correspondence. |
Revolutionaries—France—Correspondence. |
Intellectuals—France—Correspondence. | France—History—Revolution,
1789–1799—Sources. | France—Intellectual life—18th century—Sources.
Classification: LCC DC146.C7 (ebook) | LCC DC146.C7 A4 2020 (print) |
DDC 944.04092 [B]—dc23
LC record available at https://lccn.loc.gov/2018038479

*This book is dedicated with admiration
and gratitude to the memory of:
Eileen O'Neill (1953–2017)*

CONTENTS

PART I

INTRODUCTION

PART II

TRANSLATION: LETTERS TO C***,
ON *THE THEORY OF MORAL SENTIMENTS*

CONTENTS

PART II

TRANSLATION: LETTERS TO C***,
ON *THE THEORY OF MORAL SENTIMENTS*

SERIES EDITORS' FOREWORD

Oxford New Histories of Philosophy (ONHP) speaks to a new climate in philosophy.

There is a growing awareness that philosophy's past is richer and more diverse than previously understood. It has become clear that canonical figures are best studied in a broad context. More exciting still is the recognition that our philosophical heritage contains long-forgotten innovative ideas, movements, and thinkers. Sometimes these thinkers warrant serious study in their own right; sometimes their importance resides in the conversations they helped reframe or problems they devised; often their philosophical proposals force us to rethink long-held assumptions about a period or genre; and frequently they cast well-known philosophical discussions in a fresh light.

There is also a mounting sense among philosophers that our discipline benefits from a diversity of perspectives and a commitment to inclusiveness. In a time when questions about justice, inequality, dignity, education, discrimination, and climate (to name a few) are especially vivid, it is appropriate to mine historical texts for insights that can shift conversations and reframe solutions. Given that philosophy's very long history contains astute discussions of a vast array of topics, the time is right to cast a broad historical net.

Lastly, there is increasing interest among philosophy instructors in speaking to the diversity and concerns of their students. Although historical discussions and texts can serve as a powerful means of doing so, finding the necessary time and tools to excavate long-buried historical materials is challenging.

Oxford New Histories of Philosophy is designed to address all these needs. It will contain new editions and translations of significant historical texts. These primary materials will make available, often for the first time, ideas and works by women, people of color, and movements in philosophy's past that were groundbreaking in their day, but left out of traditional accounts. Informative introductions will help instructors and students navigate the new material. Alongside its primary texts, ONHP will also publish monographs and collections of essays that offer philosophically subtle analyses of understudied topics, movements, and figures. In combining primary materials and astute philosophical analyses, ONHP will make it easier for philosophers, historians, and instructors to include in their courses and research exciting new materials drawn from philosophy's past.

ONHP's range will be wide, both historically and culturally. The series plans to include, for example, the writings of African American philosophers, twentieth-century Mexican philosophers, early modern and late medieval women, Islamic and Jewish authors, and nonwestern thinkers. It will excavate and analyze problems and ideas that were prominent in their day but forgotten by later historians. And it will serve as a significant aid to philosophers in teaching and researching this material.

As we expand the range of philosophical voices, it is important to acknowledge one voice responsible for this series. Eileen O'Neill was a series editor until her death, December 1, 2017. She was instrumental in motivating and conceptualizing ONHP. Her brilliant scholarship, advocacy, and generosity made all the difference to the efforts that this series is meant to represent. She will be deeply missed, as a scholar and a friend.

We are proud to contribute to philosophy's present and to a richer understanding of its past.

Christia Mercer and Melvin Rogers

Series Editors

PREFACE AND ACKNOWLEDGMENTS

Sandrine Bergès and Eric Schliesser came to Sophie de Grouchy independently—each of us has her and his own story. Bergès was giving a talk on Wollstonecraft in Montreal, and talking about her plan for writing about French women of the same period. Josiane Boulad-Ayoub brought out a copy of the *Letters*, edited by Jean-Paul Lagrave. After a suitable procrastinating delay, Bergès read the book and started contacting other scholars who might know a bit more about this fascinating philosopher: Deirdre Dawson, who generously sent her a copy of several of her articles on Grouchy, and of the edition of the *Letters* she co-edited with Marc-André Bernier; Madeleine Arnold Tétard, the author of a biography of Grouchy, who shared her knowledge of her life and times, and more preciously, perhaps, of the location of relevant historical papers; and last but not least, Eric Schliesser, who was already making Grouchy's name known through his blog posts.

In the summer of 2006, the late Eileen O'Neill invited Schliesser to contribute a paper to an edited volume on Grouchy and evaluate her distinct "philosophical contribution." Then a junior scholar, Schliesser happily accepted the invitation and was directed to Karin Brown and James E. McClellan, who generously shared their then draft edition and translation of Grouchy's *Letters*. Evelyn Forget's publications provided a solid foundation for his research. Jennifer Saul provided Schliesser with the first public occasion to lecture on Grouchy in Sheffield's Annual Women in the History of Philosophy Lecture in 2011.

Both Bergès and Schliesser went on to write about Grouchy— Schliesser first, though a delay in publishing (the forthcoming volume is now co-edited by Marcy Lascano) meant that Bergès's article came out first. They met online, through a mutual friend, and started to work together before eventually meeting in person at a conference.

Over the last decade, we've been hearing and reading more about Grouchy from others who wish the recover, to adapt O'Neill's phrase, the disappeared ink in the history of philosophy. Before that, her work was very little known, despite its great potential as a teaching and research text. We hope that by publishing this volume we will help make it even more widely discussed, and that Grouchy will reach the place she merits in the philosophical canon.

In addition to those who introduced us to Grouchy, we are especially grateful to Andrew Janiak and Marcy Lascano, who invited us both to an important, galvanizing conference that continues to shape our scholarship, as well as Spiros Tegos, who has been a spirited interlocutor on all things Grouchy. We also thank Lisa Shapiro, Karen Detlefsen, and Marguerite Deslauriers, who have created and guided the network(s) we are both part of, as well as the editor of the current series, Christia Mercer, who is the best intellectual advocate and friendly critic one can imagine, and everyone at OUP, especially our wonderful editor, Lucy Randall. We would also like to thank Lucy Balazs for her careful reading of the final draft of the text, and Anna de Bruyckere for preparing the index. We gratefully acknowledge a grant by Zon MW, The Netherlands Organisation for Health Research and Development, which helped pay for some of the expenses associated with this project.

Finally, we thank our partners, Bill and Sarit, and children, Charlotte, Max, and Avi.

ABOUT THE AUTHORS

Sandrine Bergès is associate professor in philosophy at Bilkent University in Ankara. Her books include: *The Routledge Companion to Wollstonecraft's A Vindication of the Rights of Woman (2013)* and *A Feminist Perspective on Virtue Ethics (2014)*. She also co-edited *The Social and Political Philosophy of Mary Wollstonecraft* (2016) (with Alan Coffee).

Eric Schliesser is professor of political science at the University of Amsterdam and visiting Scholar at Chapman University. He has published a monograph, *Adam Smith: Systematic Philosopher and Public Thinker* (2017), and edited a volume, *Sympathy: A History of a Concept* (2015), both with Oxford University Press. He blogs almost daily at *Digressionsnimpressions* (https://digressionsnimpressions.typepad.com).

NOTE ON THE TEXT AND TRANSLATION

Our approach to the translation and the introduction was to take into account the relevant context in sufficient detail so as to avoid making inaccurate statements, but also to enable the reader to read the text as part of the philosophical dialogue of the late Enlightenment period. In particular, in both the translation and the introduction, we took care to cross-reference the text with other texts that Sophie de Grouchy read and sought to engage with, and which influenced both her style and her arguments. These include (in French) Rousseau, Voltaire, Montesquieu, Condorcet, and (in English) Smith, Paine, Young, and even Wollstonecraft (whose early writings she seems to have been given by her friend Dumont, at the time she was writing the *Letters on Sympathy*). Schliesser's knowledge of Smith was particularly helpful in teasing out the ways in which Sophie de Grouchy is trying to engage with Smith's views, not only in *The Theory of Moral Sentiments* but also in other works that we know she had read. More generally, we tried to identify the ways in which Grouchy engages not just with Smith but also with other actors in Enlightenment practical thought and how she sought possible references to Turgot, Necker, Beccaria, Montesquieu, Condorcet, and others. We also decided to take into account other writings by Sophie de Grouchy which were recently attributed by Bergès, which cast light on some of the arguments of the *Letters*. The biographical section benefited from Sandrine Bergès's recent archival work in the library of the Institut, in Paris, which hosts the papers of Condorcet and of his descendants.

There is, unfortunately, no manuscript available from Sophie de Grouchy, and only one edition in her lifetime. This meant that we had no editing decisions to make in preparing the translation. The first edition (1798), which we have used, is freely available on the website of the Bibliothèque Nationale de France, and there are several more or less scholarly editions available.

Translating texts from another period is always difficult, in that a happy medium must be struck between conveying the tone of the period and rendering it more readable for contemporary readers. Some arcane words had to be translated by more recent ones, and where there was no suitable translation, I added a note explaining what the word meant in its context. Here I highlight a few of the decisions I made while translating.

Grouchy, like many of her contemporaries, favored long sentences—at times covering several paragraphs before reaching a full stop. I have inserted punctuation and paragraph breaks where there were none, for the sake of readability.

As Grouchy translated Smith, and surely had his text in mind when she wrote the *Letters*, I have used, whenever possible, his terminology to translate hers. Where the number of words and expressions covering a particular concept in French and in English differed, I had to make a decision.

One particular problem we faced was that of producing a text that did not constantly use masculine terms. There are many references to "les hommes" in the original, but that text was written at a time when it was still plausible to believe that the masculine could be used at times to refer to the human race as a whole. Sometimes it made sense to translate this as simply "people." Other times, I took advantage of the fact that French assigns gender to concepts and inanimate objects more or less randomly and kept the feminine pronoun in English. So "une personne" became "she," even though it is really meant to be gender neutral.

Sandrine Bergès

SOPHIE DE GROUCHY'S *LETTERS ON SYMPATHY*

PART I

INTRODUCTION

Chapter 1

Life and Context

1.1 LIFE

Sophie de Grouchy, 1764–1822, was an aristocrat who aligned herself with the republican party of the Girondins during the revolution, translating works by Thomas Paine and writing political pieces of her own and together with her husband, Condorcet. Although most of her writings are lost, she did leave one significant work of philosophy, the *Letters on Sympathy* [hereafter, *Letters*], translated here. This work was published in 1798, together with Grouchy's translation of Adam Smith's (1759) *The Theory of Moral Sentiments* [hereafter, *TMS*] and his "A Dissertation on the Origin of Languages: or, Considerations Concerning the First Formation of Languages and the Different Genius" ([hereafter "A Dissertation"] added by Smith to the third, 1767 edition of *TMS*). The *Letters* were advertised as a commentary on *TMS*.

Sophie de Grouchy was born in 1764 at the castle of Villette, near Meulan, a land that had been in her family since Louis XV. The family was of Norman extraction, with some ancestors traveling with William the Conqueror and others in St. Louis's (Louis IX) crusades. One ancestor, Nicolas de Grouchy, had been tutor to Montaigne. Sophie's family was a literary one. They spent the winter seasons in Paris in a *hôtel particulier* (a residential palace) where they hosted

3

the intellectual elite of the day: Turgot, d'Alembert, Beaumarchais, Condorcet.

Grouchy's education benefited from this general atmosphere. Although she did not have a tutor of her own, she was allowed to join her brothers' studies, so that she learned English, Latin, Italian, and German. When the tutor was ill or away, Sophie took over from him and taught her brothers. Her bedtime reading of choice was Marcus Aurelius, whose *Meditations* were then regarded as sound reading for Christians. Her mother, who had a reputation for learning and intellect, ensured that her children's education was not merely cerebral: she regularly took Grouchy and her sister, Charlotte, on charity rounds to visit the poor and the sick, teaching how to help and to comfort, and how to value the well-being of others. In the argument of the *Letters*, this experience is treated as formative.

When she turned eighteen, Grouchy was sent to the Chanoinesse school of Neuville, an ostensibly religious establishment, but mostly a finishing school for very rich and very well connected aristocratic girls and women. There she partied and studied equally hard, damaging her eyesight in the process. In the evenings the Chanoinesses hosted balls, and in the day, while the others recovered from the night's excesses, Sophie practiced her languages and put them to good use translating works from English and Italian—all fashionably political works, such as Arthur Young's *Tour in Ireland* and Tasso's *Liberation of Jerusalem*. She also read, discovering Voltaire, Diderot, and especially Rousseau. She lost her faith, but her early training in Christian charity, with her mother showing her how good it felt to relieve others' trouble, blended with her new readings, turned her toward social justice.

Through her readings, Grouchy also became a republican—several years before Robespierre even contemplated the possibility of a French republic. She was not yet concerned with the question of the administration of the country—although, like her husband, she later became in favor of representative, rather than direct, democracy. Her focus at that time was with eradicating the psychological distance between the rich and the poor, wanting everyone to be a citizen, not a subject, and no one so rich or powerful that he could become a tyrant. This orientation is reflected in the *Letters*, where her political discussion is primarily focused on the psychological effects of oppression and inequality on the flourishing of the population.

Coming home to Villette, Grouchy announced to her horrified mother that she had become an atheist. Madame de Grouchy responded by burning all of Grouchy's Rousseau, Voltaire, and Diderot books and bringing Marcus Aurelius—a favorite of eighteenth-century Christian Deists—out again. Every night Grouchy would pray that God may give her back her faith—until it became obvious that he would not oblige, and she gave up. Fortunately for her, she was still much loved and valued, not just by her immediate family but also by her uncle and aunt, Charles and Félicité Dupaty, who put her in charge of their son, Charles Mercier Dupaty's education. Through her uncle, she developed further her passion for social justice; he was a magistrate and fought to reform the French criminal system, which punished the poor heavily and unfairly, while letting the rich get away. Uncle and niece saw eye to eye on this and greatly admired each other. At that time, the uncle was fighting the *parlements* (provincial appellate courts) to put a stop to the condemnation of three peasants from Bordeaux to torture on the wheel. He was working on this with the Marquis de Condorcet.[1]

Sophie met Condorcet through her uncle. They already had much in common, both being republicans and atheists. But while Condorcet could express his convictions, Grouchy was still somewhat under the control of her family. This must have made Condorcet an

---

1. Ian McLean and Fiona Hewitt, eds., *Condorcet: Foundations of Social Choice and Political Theory* (Cheltenham: Edward Elgar, 1994), 17.

attractive party, despite the age difference—she was twenty-two, he was forty-three. Her intellect and her ability to hold her own in political debates with her uncle would no doubt have pleased Condorcet, but he also found out that she was brave and devoted. One day her tutee was attacked by a rabid dog: Sophie threw herself between the young Charles and the beast. Condorcet admired her from a safe distance, and soon the two were engaged and, in 1786, were married.

They moved to Condorcet's apartments in the Hotel des Monnaies; Condorcet worked as the Inspector-General of the Mint, under the economist Turgot. There the couple set up a salon. Grouchy's English was excellent by then, so theirs was the house of choice for foreign visitors, such as Thomas Jefferson, Thomas Paine, Anarchasis Cloots, and the Swiss Etienne Dumont—speechwriter for Mirabeau and translator of Jeremy Bentham. Their devoted friend, the doctor Pierre-Jean-George Cabanis, who later married Grouchy's sister, Charlotte, was a frequent attendant.

Grouchy did not stop studying after she married. Shortly after she moved into the Hotel des Monnaies, Condorcet together with another Academician, La Harpe, founded the Lycée, a school on the rue St. Honoré, where famous scholars and academicians lectured, and where the cream of society attended. Grouchy participated assiduously, studying mathematics, history, and botany. She became known as the Venus of the Lyceum—presumably because she was good-looking. She also took lessons in painting in the studio of Elizabeth Vigée le Brun. Grouchy painted well, as we know from the several miniatures she left behind, including several self-portraits.

At the start of the French Revolution (1789), the Condorcets became associated with the Girondins. They frequented the salon of Madame Helvetius, in Auteuil, where republican ideas were being debated and Brissot's anti-slavery club (of which Condorcet and Olympe de Gouges were members) was founded. By 1791, Grouchy and Condorcet were among the strongest advocates of the republican movement, working with Thomas Paine, Jacques-Pierre Brissot, Etienne Dumont, and Achilles Duchatellet, on *Le Républicain*, a newspaper that would disseminate republican thought in France. But by 1793, the Girondins fell out of favor and Condorcet had to go into hiding. He stayed in Paris while Grouchy moved to Auteuil—then outside Paris—with her daughter, traveling to the capital on foot twice a week to visit her husband and to paint in a studio she had rented on the rue St. Honoré. In March 1794, Condorcet fled his hiding place in order to avoid getting his hostess arrested. He died a few days later in a village prison, but was not identified until several months after his death, so that Grouchy remained ignorant of his whereabouts.

As Grouchy struggled to regain some of the property that had been confiscated and at the same time keep herself out of prison, she earned a living using the skills she had acquired as a miniaturist, painting portraits of imprisoned aristocrats for their families and, on two occasions, those of officers coming to arrest her. By the time the Terror was over, and she still had not regained control of her property, she decided to earn money by translating Adam Smith's *The Theory of Moral Sentiments (TMS)*. She took this opportunity to publish her *Letters on Sympathy*, written several years earlier, as an afterword. She also worked on two editions of the complete works of Condorcet, together with Cabanis, and continued to educate herself and develop her thoughts in areas as varied as physiology and botany.

Grouchy died in 1822, age fifty-eight. Her daughter, Eliza, who had married an Irish man and revolutionary sympathizer, Alexander O'Connor, inherited her father's papers and, together with François Arago, an important academician and life-long republican, she completed the editions of Condorcet's work her mother had prepared, and published a new edition of his *Works*. It was Eliza's son who commissioned biographer Antoine Guillois to write a life of Sophie de

Grouchy. This is our main source for details concerning her life, as her papers have mostly disappeared.

1.2 ADAM SMITH IN FRANCE

Although the *Letters* were written before Grouchy translated *TMS*, they are framed, in part, as a response to that book, so that it makes sense to say a few words about Adam Smith's reception in France, and the significance of Grouchy's having chosen this work to engage with.

Smith was in fact very popular in France, especially with his (1776) *Inquiry into the Nature and Causes of the Wealth of Nations* (hereafter *Wealth of Nations*), having been translated five times already between 1776 and 1786.[2] This was due to the French reading public's thirst for sound reflections on economics and taxation, for the pressing need for an applied philosophy that could help them out of the terrible economic crisis they had fallen into. Smith's *TMS*, however, did not do so well, despite having been translated several times. Smith blamed the fact that the book did not sell in France as much as he'd expected on the poor quality of the translation, which "greatly mortified" him.[3]

It is not entirely surprising that Smith had issues with the translations produced by Eidous (1764), La Rochefoucauld (1774), and Blavet (1774–75). Translating practices in eighteenth-century France were "domesticating" practices—that is, emphasis was placed on making the text fit with local canons and debates, and less on making sure the author's meaning was conveyed exactly and in a way he

---

2. Gilbert Faccarello and Philippe Steiner, "The Diffusion of the Work of Adam Smith in the French Language: An Outline History," in *A Critical Bibliography of Adam Smith*, ed. Keith Tribe (London: Pickering and Chatto, 2002), 61–119.

3. See Faccarello and Steiner, "The Diffusion," 10. Smith could read French, although he was not comfortable speaking it.

or she intended it.[4] So, for instance, the original text was summarized if it was thought too long, or examples were added if the text was thought too dry—fidelity to the original was not the first concern. And whereas this apparently did no harm to the popularity of the *Wealth of Nations*, it did affect the sales of the French translations of *TMS*.

Smith was no longer alive by the time Grouchy published her own translation (1798; he died in 1790), but it is safe to say that he would have been happier with hers, as she followed the text as precisely as she could, attempting to capture the tone and rhythm, as well as the multilayered meanings of his sentences. Moreover, Grouchy translated the seventh and final edition of *The Theory of Moral Sentiments*, which was published posthumously. This is no doubt a large part of why her translation lasted longer than others (the next translation, by Bizioux et al., was published in 1999).

Did Grouchy ever meet Smith? She does not suggest that they did in her *Letters*. Her biographer, Guillois, names Smith as one of the international visitors to her Paris Salon. In fact, although Condorcet and Smith knew of each other, it is unlikely that Grouchy and Smith ever met.[5] Even though Smith traveled to France, he does not seem to have been in Paris at a time when he could have met Grouchy.

4. Mary Helen McMurran, *The Spread of Novels: Translation and Prose Fiction in the Eighteenth Century* (Princeton, NJ: Princeton University Press, 2009), 3. On the controversy over André Morellet's translation of Beccaria, an important influence on Grouchy, see Eric Schliesser, "On Philosophical Translator-Advocates and Linguistic Injustice," *Philosophical Papers* 47(1), (2018): 20–22.

5. Simona Pisanelli, "Adam Smith and the Marquis de Condorcet: Did They Really Meet?," *Iberian Journal for the History of Economic Thought*, 2 (2015). http://revistas.ucm.es/index.php/IJHE/article/view/49771/46266. However, Smith and Condorcet did correspond, and Condorcet presented Smith with a copy of his *Life of Turgot* (1786). Peter Groenewegen, "Turgot and Adam Smith," *Scottish Journal of Political Economy* 16, no. 3 (1969): 271–287, 271.

1.3 SOURCES

Not unlike other authors in this period, Grouchy does not much cite her sources. In the text of the *Letters*, only Smith, Locke, Voltaire, Rousseau, Fénelon, and Vauvenargues are explicitly mentioned. In addition, she quotes Condorcet once without explicitly identifying him. In the footnotes to the translation, we identify a few other possible intellectual interlocutors and sources, including works by Montesquieu, Hume, Marcus Aurelius, Beccaria, Turgot, and Bentham.

Of the ones she mentions explicitly, English-language contemporary readers are unlikely to recognize Fénelon and Vauvenargues. So, here we start with them and in our discussion introduce some of the others.

First, François Fénelon (1651–1715) was, prior to his political fall, one of the most influential clerics, theologians, and educators in France. He is mentioned at the end of Letter IV as a way to praise Rousseau's rhetoric of virtue ("Rousseau talked of virtue with as much charm as Fenelon"). It is almost certainly an allusion to Fénelon's (1699) *Les Aventures de Télémaque* (*The Adventures of Telemachus*), one of the most famous works during the eighteenth century.[6] A common interpretation of the work is that it defends rural republican virtue; it helped set off the so-called luxury debate. On one side of the debate were those who believed that commerce and luxury corrupt our morals and—with a nod to the Roman civil wars and the decline of the Republic—undermine political stability and freedom. Fénelon was frequently taken to be an advocate of this

---

6. The complicated publication history of the text is itself part of the story of Fénelon's fall. For an introduction to the text, the context, and a nuanced interpretation of its significance, see Ryan Patrick Hanley, "Fénelon's *Telemachus*," in *Ten Neglected Classics of Philosophy*, ed. Eric Schliesser (Oxford: Oxford University Press, 2016), 26–54.

position. On the other side of the debate were those who believed that commerce and luxury would lead to national military and economic greatness; if this meant an embrace of vice, so be it. The Anglo-Dutch writer Bernard Mandeville, whose *Fable of the Bees* was a direct response to Fénelon, was a leading representative.[7]

Much political and moral philosophy and political economy of the eighteenth century is an attempt to do justice to the insights of Fénelon and Mandeville, while avoiding their conclusions. So, for example, Hume and Smith both argued, influenced by Montesquieu, that commerce could produce not just national greatness but, with the right institutions, also better morals.[8] Smith argued that one could tax luxury consumption by the rich so as to fund the provision of public works that benefit all. Addison and Kant (presumably unknown to Grouchy) both argued, more optimistically, that commerce would facilitate international peace. With those that advocate commerce, Grouchy evinces familiarity with arguments offered by Turgot and Smith that show restrictions on and barriers to commerce have a tendency to act as a monopoly for the few that impoverish the many. Her argument against monopoly is not merely economic but also political: "those laws, at the same time, were harming the well-being of all by collecting, little by little, in the hands of a few, wealth that then became in those hands a means of oppression, and which otherwise, through the free movement of interests would have remained if not equal, at least common to all." Not unlike Smith, she thinks that free markets have an equalizing tendency. This is a natural thought when the status quo is deeply hierarchical and in which the

---

7. For an excellent introduction to these issues, see Istvan Hont, "The Early Enlightenment Debate on Commerce and Luxury," in *The Cambridge History of Eighteenth-Century Political Thought*, ed. Mark Goldie and Robert Wokler (Cambridge: Cambridge University Press, 2006), 377–418.

8. See, for example, Lisa Herzog, "Adam Smith on Markets and Justice," *Philosophy Compass* 9, no. 12 (2014): 864–875.

aristocratic rich have economic and tax privileges (so that they avoid paying taxes) and deeply entrenched legal exemptions. Privileges and exemptions do not just have an economic and political effect, however. In Letter VIII, Grouchy argues that these also undermine the impartial rule of law and threaten its authority, because they convey the thought to those subject to it that even the criminal law itself is an instrument of the rich against the poor: "the people are tempted to see criminal laws as made against them and in favor of the rich, as the result of an association designed to oppress them." (Grouchy here seems to draw an implicit contrast between an illegitimate association and a legitimate union.) She argues that one of the unintended, but foreseeable, consequences of laws that favor the wealthy is that of increasing contempt for the law and so increasing lawlessness.

To be sure, Grouchy's views should not be assimilated fully to Smith's political economy. At one point (in Letter VII), she endorses a set of physiocratic doctrines: "agriculture is, after all, the most productive of all professions for individuals, while for states, it is the unique source of real and lasting wealth." As a systematic political economy, physiocracy was founded by Quesnay (1694–1774) and was embraced, as a reaction to Colbert's *dirigiste* form of mercantilism, by many of the modernizing French *philosophes*, including Turgot, who developed his political economy in the context of a larger argument about progress (which surely influenced Condorcet). Physiocrats advocated free trade as the best means to prevent famines and aimed to develop the impoverished French countryside. While Smith admired Quesnay and Turgot, in Book IV of *Wealth of Nations*, he attacked mercantilism and physiocracy as promoting one-sided economic development. Grouchy was apparently unconvinced by Smith's argument.

Earlier we mentioned how Fénelon and Mandeville represented opposing sides of the luxury debate. But this opposition was not total; their views were taken to be in agreement on a crucial element: if left unsupervised, the working poor were profligate and lazy. This helped justify a whole range of economic policies, including what we would call "sin taxes" on the consumption goods by the poor and maintenance of low wages (in order to motivate the poor to work hard). Grouchy echoed Smith in rejecting the assumptions behind and the content of such policies, and instead favored policies that would enrich the poor. She thought the working poor were not naturally profligate. In addition, any "mismatch" between their "wages" and "the necessities of life" would be "temporary" suggesting she accepted Smith's argument that the necessities of life of the work poor created an important link between the price level, the wages of the working poor, and population size (Letter VII).

She argues that laws, which target the behavior of the poor, create perverse incentives, which impoverish the poor and encourage criminality. Many of Grouchy's particular arguments on legal reform are original. But they reveal the more general influence not just of Smith but also, and specifically, of the great Italian legal reformer (and political economist) Cesare Beccaria (1738–1794), who was extremely influential on French Enlightenment thought. In Beccaria we find some of the eclectic and, to modern eyes, curious mixture of state-of-nature theorizing (that modern readers associate with Hobbes, Locke, and Rousseau) and utilitarianism (that moderns associate with Hutcheson, Helvetius, Bentham, and sometimes Hume) that we can also find in Grouchy.

As well as Beccaria, Grouchy may have read or discussed Jeremy Bentham. Her friend and correspondent, Etienne Dumont, was Bentham's editor and his translator into French. We know that when Dumont was working with Bentham in England, he corresponded with Grouchy; and while we do not have his letters to her, we do know from her replies that Bentham was discussed. This correspondence dates from the same time as the first drafting of the *Letters,* and we should not be surprised, therefore, to find some elements of Bentham's thought in the *Letters*.

While there is some evidence that Grouchy was familiar with Bentham's early works, the main notion of "utility" that she deploys is, in fact, a bit closer to Beccaria, Hutcheson, Helvetius, and Hume. In that sense, "utility" means something like "public good" (sometimes she uses "common utility" or "general utility" to capture notions related to this). Not unlike Smith, she clearly evaluates social institutions like the law in such consequentialist terms. The main consequences that matter are pleasure and virtue. She thinks that such utility can come in degrees (see Letter VIII). But unlike Bentham, she does not offer a calculus nor does she aim to maximize the utility of individuals.

One may wonder, then, why Grouchy avoids the welfare-maximizing calculus of Bentham. While one can only speculate, it seems this is due to the fact that, not unlike Smith, she thinks utility may be one of several competing values, none of which has ultimate priority.[9] For at times, she thinks that even institutions should be evaluated in light of "reason," by which she means, in this context, impartiality (e.g., Letter VIII: "when they considered that reason and common utility were the natural and absolute judges of social institutions"). We offer two further comments on Grouchy's conception of utility.

First, she treats utility as something that an individual can have in relationship to another individual: "we now see how we are disposed to a particular sympathy for those we are tied to by utility or pleasure" (Letter II). Here she uses utility as an explanation for a directed sympathy with somebody else. That is, if another is—because of her, say, riches, influence, or status—useful to us, we are likely to feel sympathy for her. Again, this is unlike the Benthamite notion where utility

---

9. Michael B. Gill, "Moral Pluralism in Smith and His Contemporaries," *Revue internationale de philosophie* 3 (2014): 275–306.

is related to a hedonic or psychological property of experience. (As it happens, Grouchy helpfully distinguishes utility from pleasure in the quoted passage.)

Second, her main conception of utility is relevant when it comes to her sole mention of Vauvenargues (1715–1747), who is even less well known today than Fénelon. Vauvenargues, an aristocrat, was also little known in his own short lifetime, but he was befriended by Voltaire, who drew attention to his writings. In Letter V, Grouchy quotes Vauvenargues as holding that "moral good and evil refer to whatever is more useful or harmful to humanity in general." The idea that "good" just is what is useful can be traced back to Hobbes and Spinoza. But the idea that this should be understood in terms of humanity in general seems original to Vauvenargues. It presupposes a cosmopolitan understanding of the public good. Not unlike Grouchy, Stoicism greatly influenced Vauvenargues in his youth, although there is debate about his mature views.[10] Proto-utilitarians (like Hutcheson, Helvetius, and Beccaria) tend to treat such utility in terms of the greatest number, not in terms of humanity as such.

Grouchy mentions Vauvenargues in order to contrast his conception of good and evil with her own conception of *moral* evil: "that is of an act that is harmful to others and which is prohibited by reason." Grouchy here presupposes a distinction between moral and physical pains. The contrast between the "moral" and "physical" was a standard one in the second half of the eighteenth century. The "physical" refers to bodies or matter—so, "physical evils" are bodily pains. The "moral" refers to what we would call "social," but it used to refer to things connected to the mind (in a broad sense)—so, a "moral evil" is a social harm.

<hr>

10. Yves Lainey, "Vauvenargues and his Work," *Theoria: A Journal of Social and Political Theory* 27 (1966): 21–30.

Grouchy's criticism of Vauvenargues is a bit complex. In part, he is treated as a misguided elitist who fails to see that the working poor are capable of sound moral evaluation. But her grounds for criticizing Vauvenargues are themselves a bit elitist: that the working poor will lack understanding of such a cosmopolitan conception of humanity in general. She states the point, however, in an egalitarian way: "we should prefer those definitions that the least enlightened of men may grasp." (Grouchy here echoes Smith's criticism of Hume in *TMS* IV, where Smith shows that disinterested utility could not ground the origin of an institution it is meant to justify because it is too "refined and enlightened.") The underlying point is a serious one. She rejects a kind of elitist-moral expertise: the most reliable and enlightened reason is that which is the most common.

The other reason for calling her criticism "complex" is that while criticizing Vauvenargues's definition, Grouchy also claims that, in fact, their definitions actually agree. That is, there is a sense in which their definitions are meant to track a common (and cosmopolitan) good (or evil). This turns on her understanding of reason, which— to simplify—is not just a psychological faculty that can calculate the foreseeable effects or outcomes of actions but also a kind of cosmopolitan principle that demands from us that we are all treated equally, or impartially. So, a moral evil is a harm to others when that violates this cosmopolitan principle. Putting it this way allows her to avoid calling, say, momentary or instrumental social dislocations "evil."

The impact of two of the towering figures of the French Enlightenment, Voltaire and Rousseau, on her *Letters* is more diffuse, and we cannot hope to do justice to this in the confines of an introduction. Voltaire is explicitly quoted when she begins to introduce her views on moral education in Letter I. But Grouchy's views on how to organize institutions and individual practices of education into virtue also reveal she was a close, albeit critical student of Rousseau's *Emile*. She shares a republican conception of virtue with

Rousseau, but the *Letters* are framed by her rejection of his sexism toward women.

Letter IV closes with an extended contrast between Rousseau and Voltaire. She treats them as exemplars of certain kinds of rhetorically sophisticated public intellectuals: one who speaks for freedom (Rousseau), and the other who speaks for public enlightenment (Voltaire). The treatment of Rousseau is simultaneously more critical and more admiring: Rousseau speaks to our conscience in a way that flirts with demagoguery (because it works by way of the emotions). But unlike demagogues, Rousseau ends up avoiding flattery of his audience and "disciplines" our hearts and orients us toward public virtue. Voltaire, by contrast, effectively uses ridicule to undermine the power of religious institutions and other sources of fanaticism and superstition. She shares with Voltaire an anti-clerical animus.

There is a subtle point lurking in the main contrast between Rousseau and Voltaire. Like other Enlightenment figures, Grouchy draws on a stadial conception of history hinted at in Mandeville, but most subtly articulated by Montesquieu and Buffon, and later developed in the Scottish Enlightenment (including Hume and Smith). At some point, this stadial conception of history became understood as a template for progress. Not unlike Turgot and Condorcet, Grouchy thinks that once Enlightenment spreads, it is permanent; so, future ages do not need a new Voltaire. In contrast, she also believes that freedom can be threatened in each age, and so Rousseau's works will always remain relevant and, due to their emotional nature, potentially effective.

1.4 WOMEN PHILOSOPHERS IN THE REVOLUTION

Despite what many hoped, the French Revolution did not liberate women. In fact, they were probably worse off at the end of the revolution than they had been during the Ancience Régime, when they were at least included in public life and often were a force to be reckoned with.[11] Yet, the revolutionary years saw a massive increase in publications by women in France. Between 1789 and 1800, there were a total of 329 publications written by women. In the previous three decades, the numbers ranged between 55 and 78. And between 1811 and 1821, it decreased to 299 (presumably because many of the writers of the revolutionary years had been guillotined).[12] Carla Hesse, whose figures these are, reports that in England, while there was a regular increase of women in print, it was not as dramatic as in France. Between 1780 and 1789, 166 women were published, and the following decade, it was 191.[13] English women writers were to some extent encouraged by the Revolution, especially if they were republican thinkers—as, for example, were Wollstonecraft, Barbauld, and Macaulay. These women were prompted to action both by the fact that republicanism was becoming a real possibility and the implication that French women might, with some help, be included in the reforms taking shape. Writers who had thought about the possibility of women's citizenship, such as Wollstonecraft and Macaulay, had understood the role of institutions, as well as of laws and individuals, in dominating women's actions. Women were held down not just by laws but also by social habits, prejudices, and practices, which made it nearly impossible for a woman to rise up and stay up long enough to require citizenship.

11. See Carla Hesse, *The Other Enlightenment: How French Women Became Modern* (Princeton, NJ: Princeton University Press, 2001), 32. Olympe de Gouges, in her "Declaration of the Rights of Woman," refers to women's "nocturnal administration," meaning that many political decisions were made by influential wives and especially mistresses. For the impact on scholarship, see the seminal paper by Eileen O'Neill, "Disappearing Ink: Early Modern Women Philosophers and Their Fate in History," in *Philosophy in a Feminist Voice: Critiques and Reconstructions*, ed. Janet A. Kourany (Princeton, NJ: Princeton University Press, 1998), 17–62.
12. Hesse, *The Other Enlightenment*, 37.
13. Hesse, *The Other Enlightenment*, 39.

Women writers in France (Olympe de Gouges, Etta Palm D'Aelders) did also take to the Revolution and attempted to convince the new rulers that women should be granted citizenship. Some (Madame de Staël, Louise Kéralio Robert), however, preferred to use their influence to help men become citizens. Grouchy's husband, Condorcet, was one of the most active advocates of women's rights. In 1790, he published a paper arguing that women should be given rights of citizenship on the same basis as men, because nothing else would serve equality.[14] In this paper, he lists a number of objections that had been or might be presented regarding the inclusion of women in politics; he debunks them, one after another. He concludes by naming a number of famous intellectual or political women, daring anyone to argue that they would not make better political leaders than most men. There is no reason to suspect that Grouchy had a hand in writing this piece, but we know that they had a close marriage and discussed their work together, as well as with friends in their salon and in that of Madame Helvétius. A few months later, Condorcet introduced the Dutch exile Etta Palm D'Aelders to his Cercle Social, and had a paper of hers published, also arguing for the inclusion of women as citizens in the new republic. D'Aelders then went on to create several patriotic societies for women citizens throughout France.[15]

It is not clear to what extent Grouchy participated in her husband's activism, however. Condorcet was always cautious. When his wife and infant daughter got caught up in the Champ de Mars massacre, in the summer of 1791, Condorcet immediately closed down

14. Nicolas de Condorcet, "Sur l'Admission des Femmes au droits de la cite," *Journal of the Society of 1789*, July 3, 1790; Nicolas de Condorcet, "On the Emancipation of Women," in *Condorcet: Political Writings*, ed. Steven Lukes and Nadia Urbinati (Cambridge: Cambridge University Press, 2012), 156–162.
15. See Elisabeth Badinter and Robert Badinter, *Condorcet: Un Intellectuel en Politique* (Paris: Fayard, 1988), 297.

the journal they had just started together, *Le Républicain*, for fear that someone would come after his family.[16] Grouchy, as an outspoken republican aristocrat and an attractive young woman, was already the subject of much malicious gossip. It is not unlikely that Condorcet decided he would be the one to promote a view as unpopular as women's citizenship. Although there are hints of Grouchy's feminism in the *Letters on Sympathy*, there is nothing analogous to her husband's clearly stated feminist agenda.

Condorcet was right to be cautious. Although women's active participation in the Revolution was tolerated at first, their involvement was later violently repressed. Women who had interested themselves in politics and had written about it, such as Olympe de Gouges and Marie-Jeanne Roland, were executed in 1793, whereas Grouchy lived until 1822. It's likely that the backlash was always going to happen, but the incident that seems to have sparked it was the (1793) murder of Marat by Charlotte Corday, a young Girondin sympathizer who had come to Paris to kill a monster and save the revolution. Shortly after her execution, which was closely followed by Roland's and Gouges's executions, Hébert issued the following warning to women in *Le Moniteur*, a leading publication of the Terror:

> Women, do you want to be republicans? Love, follow and teach the laws that remind your children to exercise their rights. Have glory in the brilliant actions they may one day perform on behalf of the fatherland, because these speak well of you; be simple in your dress, laborious in your household work; never follow popular assemblies with the aim of speaking there; but by your occasional presence at them, encourage your children to participate;

16. See Grouchy and Duchatelet's letters to Dumont on this subject, in Jean Martin, "Achille du Chastellet et le Premier Mouvement Républicain en France d'Après des Lettres Inédites (1791–1792)," in *La Revolution Française, Revue Historique*, Nouvelle série 33 (Paris: L. Maretheux, Imprimeur de la Cour d'Appel, 1927), 116.

then your fatherland will bless you, because you will truly have done for it what it expects of you.[17]

Women's clubs were closed, and there was no more talk of women acquiring the same rights as men. Then, when Napoléon came to power, he is reported to have told Sophie de Grouchy that he did not like women who talked about politics. She replied, echoing a famous argument by Olympe de Gouges: "I agree with you, but in a country where they might lose their heads, it is natural that women should want to know why."

17. Dauban, Charles Aimé. 1864. Etude sur Madame Roland et son temps. Paris: Plon, ccxlix. Sandrine Bergès' translation.

Chapter 2

The Text

2.1 WRITING THE *LETTERS*

The *Letters on Sympathy* were published in year six of the new French First Republic—that is, in 1798. They were appended to a two-volume translation of Adam Smith's *TMS* and "A Dissertation." Perhaps the new translation was encouraged by the appearance of a French translation of Smith's posthumous (1795) *Essays on Philosophical Subjects* by the Suisse natural philosopher, Pierre Prévost; this showed there was interest in Smith's works in French.

While the *Letters* were published in 1798, we have good reasons to believe that they were written in 1793, with drafts prepared in 1791. First, Condorcet refers to them in his testament (written in the early days of 1794), suggesting to his daughter that for her moral and philosophical education, she should turn to her mother's *Letters on Sympathy*, as well as to "other fragments on the same subject." We do not know what these other texts might have been, or whether they were developed beyond fragments between Condorcet's death in 1794 and Grouchy's in 1822.

In fact, Grouchy herself referred to the *Letters* at an even earlier date. In the spring of 1792, in correspondence with Etienne Dumont, their Swiss friend and associate, she asked whether he would look at a draft of seven "letters," adding that she could not find the draft of the eighth and final one. She also mentioned the draft of a novel with which she was not satisfied. Later, she wrote Dumont another letter, berating him for not offering any feedback (despite the offer of a dinner) and adding that it would have cost him very little indeed to say whether he thought there was anything in them that was worth pursuing.[1]

We do not know whether she eventually found someone, other than her husband, to read the draft, or whether the novel was abandoned. But we do know why the *Letters* were eventually published in 1798. According to Grouchy's daughter, Eliza Condorcet O'Connor, Sophie published her translation of Adam Smith's works because she needed money. Her assets had been confiscated, and it was taking a long time to get them back. She needed to live and to pay for her daughter's upkeep, as well as an annuity for her nanny and help for her sister.

Montesquieu's *Persian Letters* published in 1721 had repopularized the epistolary format. Grouchy's approach is closer to Seneca's *Letters* (1917), which are instructive and have a dedicated addressee whose responses are not recorded (or only obliquely hinted at). A remark at the start of Letter III suggests that each letter is meant to be a daily missive. The headings on Letters V–VII suggest that they are a connected argument.

Although the epistolary format is a stylistic choice, and the "letters" work as the chapters of a short treatise; they are all addressed to a reader, and the introductions and conclusions all appeal to that reader's judgment of the arguments presented. This might suggest that Grouchy is setting up her reader as an intellectual version of Smith's "impartial spectator"—someone who is to provide an

---

1. Martin, "Achille du Chastellet," 121.

objective judgment. The concept of the impartial spectator is notice-ably absent from the argument of the *Letters*, so it would not be entirely surprising to find that Grouchy had somehow worked it into the fabric of her text.

The recipient of each letter is not named; all are addressed to "My dear C***." Some have surmised that C*** stood for Condorcet. However, as he was dead by the time the *Letters* were published, that is highly unlikely. Although he was alive when the *Letters* were drafted, it is also unlikely she would have thought to present her work as a correspondence with her husband, as they were living together then and in the public eye. The only surviving correspondence we have between the couple was written while Condorcet was in hiding. There was, on the other hand, another C*** with whom Grouchy cor-responded and collaborated throughout her adult life: Jean-Georges Cabanis, a close friend of the Condorcets; the lover and later the husband of Charlotte de Grouchy, Sophie's sister; and a favorite of Madame Helvetius.

Cabanis (1757–1808), whose father had been one of Turgot's assistants, was an influential physician and theorist of what we would today call public health. He had a common interest with Grouchy—namely, physiology, which was a materialist science aimed at understanding human beings by way of their bodily organs. In 1802, Cabanis published his *Rapports du Physique et du Moral de l'Homme*, in which he explored the relations between bod-ies and morality, discussing, for instance, the influence of weather and digestion on mood and decision-making. Prior to publish-ing this, he corresponded with Grouchy and had long discussions with her on the subject. Physiology is also central to the *Letters on Sympathy*, as Grouchy argues that our moral feelings are born out of the physiological response that ties a newborn to the person who nurses her and holds her.

2.2 SUMMARY OF THE *LETTERS*

In Letter I, Grouchy introduces her project—to find the origins of sympathy— and sets out her view that these origins are physiological, that they are based in pain and pleasure, whether experienced, remembered, imagined, or processed by the mind through reflection. In Letter II, she shows how reflection, memory, and abstraction lead from physical sympathy for a specific person to moral sympathy for the whole of humanity. She argues that the very first human bonds arise from the need an infant feels for the body of her nurse. The pleasure and pain experienced by the infant in relation to the presence or absence of the nurse is the first step toward the development of sympathy. As the ability to take a step back from these sensations develops, and the sensations themselves become more complex and attached to more abstract objects, sympathy matures into the sort of sentiment that can in turn give rise to morality.

Letter III expands on Letter II by offering a discussion of different kinds of sympathy, personal sympathy, friendship, and romantic love, showing how each develops from a similar basis.

Letter IV asks what it is we may feel sympathy for, and looks in particular at the infectious power of laughter and its role in psychological development. This letter, which is more loosely structured than the others, also touches on the question of the influence of demagogues and on the psychology of crowds. It forms the transition to the next four letters, where she applies her theory of sympathy to politically salient, institutional reform.

Letter V is entitled "On the Origins of Moral Ideas" and begins with an analysis of the concepts of virtue, moral goodness, evil, and remorse in light of her discussion of Smith that occurs in the previous letters. In her analysis, she moves between virtue ethical and consequentialist explanations of moral concepts. On the one hand, everything must stem from the character of the agent, which has to be educated in order to develop the propensity to feel the right sort of sympathy in the right circumstances—this is clearly Aristotelian in spirit. On the other hand, she claims that reason approves of or condemns acts depending on whether they are beneficial to humanity or not—which feels more utilitarian.

We might reflect here that at the end of the eighteenth century, although consequentialism was very new and no doubt felt revolutionary, it was not yet a stance that positioned itself against more Aristotelian perspectives. The idea that there are three different types of moral theories—Kantian, utilitarian, and Aristotelian—was very new. And, later, Mill himself claimed that his own views were not incompatible with Aristotle's. Grouchy herself was not an Aristotelian. This was not a position held by anyone at the time, even though ancient virtue ethical notions were widespread both philosophically and culturally; and Grouchy was well acquainted with Stoicism. Talk of virtue would have come naturally to her, but she also had some acquaintance with consequentialist views.

The aim of the next two letters, VI and VII, both headed with the line "The Same Subject Continued," is to derive a political economy from the moral principles outlined in Letter V. In Letter VI, Grouchy attempts to derive accounts of justice and property rights from reason and morality, showing how abstraction plays a role in mitigating the very particularistic aspect of sympathy in its original state. In Letter VII, she moves to an investigation of the mechanisms of injustice, identifying four main possible causes of unjust behavior: love, money, ambition, and vanity. In each case, she studies how the mechanics of sympathy may be interfered with so as to lead to these defects of character and reason. For instance, the sort of love, she says, that leads to crime is not the kind of love that one would naturally develop toward another human being if left to the natural movements of sympathy but, rather, is a kind perverted by unhealthy social customs and prejudices.

The final, Letter VIII, takes up where the last three left off and offers as a general conclusion that natural human sympathy and propensities toward reason, virtue, and justice have been perverted by the vicious institutions of the Ancien Régime and that these institutions must be destroyed and new ones carefully built if we are to regain the capacity for living together peacefully.

2.3 THE *LETTERS* AND *THE THEORY OF MORAL SENTIMENTS*

The *Letters on Sympathy* are introduced as a commentary and a response to Adam Smith's *The Theory of Moral Sentiments*. At several points in the *Letters*, Grouchy specifies that a particular argument constitutes a disagreement with Smith. At other times, although she does not do this, we have highlighted the disagreements in footnotes, referring the reader to the passages in Smith that we thought Grouchy was disagreeing with.

In *TMS*, Smith argues that morality arises out of the natural passions and sympathy, but that moral rules can only be developed through reason. Thus, he puts an end to the idea that either reason or sentiment by itself can give us a complete morality. The *Letters on Sympathy* especially engage with Smith's philosophical analysis of sympathy, but further than that, they have a distinct purpose, which is to bring a valuable political perspective to Smith's theory. While *TMS* is not devoid of political philosophy, it was left to Smith's readers— as had Wollstonecraft, Paine, and John Millar—to develop the full implications. In particular, Grouchy is highly interested in how understanding the mechanisms of sympathy could help the development of new social and political institutions after the revolution.

Although Grouchy is enthusiastic about Smith's views— she agrees with his fundamental view that moral sentiments and judgments can be derived from our capacity for sympathy, but that we need to develop our rational abilities in order to render this capacity at all useful—she takes issue with certain aspects of his views. In particular, and this provides the formal justification for her taking up the topic, she feels that he has not dug sufficiently deep to understand what sympathy is: he has noted "its existence and expounding its principal effects," but not gone back to "its first cause, and show why sympathy is the property of every sensible being susceptible to reflection" (Letter I). This first cause she traces back to infanthood, and to the very physical relationship of a baby with its nurse. Grouchy does not talk about mothers there, however. She is careful to distinguish between the physical relationship (skin-on-skin, feeding) and the moral one (the duty a mother may have to nurture her children, and the duties of children to love and respect their mothers). Grouchy is looking for a physical trigger for the sensations of pleasure and pain that will eventually give rise to sentiments of sympathy, and this trigger has to be common to all human beings in order to account for the ubiquitous presence of sympathy in human societies. Every baby who survives to an age at which she may develop sentiments will have been fed by an other human being, and there will have been no previous universal experience suited to stimulate the sensations that can lead to these sentiments. Thus, Grouchy not only traces sympathy back to its origins but also presents an account that is distinctly naturalistic. This bears out in her description of the growth of sympathy and the birth of morality.

Morality, for Grouchy, is first and foremost something that is felt, that has its roots in the body itself. Sentiments come first from the body, through the senses and through the experience of pleasure and pain resulting from the sense impression of a particular experience (being separated from one's nurse, or seeing one's nurse in pain or upset). The concept of "sensibility," which was extremely popular in

French Enlightenment thought,[2] itself implies a correlation between the physiological and the emotional.

When Mary Wollstonecraft criticized her century for its cultivation of sensibility, what she meant was that upper-class men and women were trained from childhood to overreact in a ridiculous fashion to a minor event—for example, to faint at the sight of a mouse, cry over nothing, or fall in love too easily. For Grouchy, though, to exercise sensibility is not that type of thing. Rather, she understands sensibility as the disposition to feel someone else's pain and pleasure. To be sure, it's sensibility with suffering and the strong desire to relieve it that is central to her approach to sympathy. (This brings her closer to Rousseau than to Smith.) For Grouchy, sensibility, or the capacity to feel pain and pleasure, is to be understood as the basis of sympathy. Someone who does not recognize pain or pleasure in himself is not likely to sense it in others. Crucially, for Grouchy, sensibility is itself something that can be cultivated (see Letter II).

Grouchy claims that there is a progression from the ability to recognize pain and pleasure in one's own body, to the ability to recognize pain and pleasure in the bodies of others, and then the ability to recognize what she calls moral—that is, psychological pain or pleasure. Grouchy is in agreement with Smith in arguing that sympathy is a complex emotion, which contains a number of judgments about who the person is, the pain he or she experiences, and whether the individual deserves that pain or not. Grouchy points out that the process whereby sensibility—the reaction to seeing somebody's pain or pleasure—becomes sympathy requires education. Unlike sensibility, sympathy is not a preexisting condition that can be either refined or blunted by social practices; rather, it is a complex emotion that requires intellectual input and, in turn, knowledge about people

2. Jessica Riskin, *Science in the Age of Sensibility: The Sentimental Empiricists of the French Enlightenment* (Chicago: University of Chicago Press, 2002).

and the ways they suffer, as well as the ability to think rapidly and abstractly about the complexity of human life.[3] Therefore, Grouchy argues, practical and theoretical education is necessary for the development of sympathy.

An important difference between Smith's and Grouchy's accounts is that for Smith, the disposition to sympathize arises out of the experience of being judged by others in childhood, whereas for Grouchy, it develops from the first relationship an infant experiences. According to her, infants learn to depend on someone to satisfy their needs, and then they learn to communicate with that person to make it easier for them to do so—that is, they cry until they get fed. This means that the first lesson must be that when we suffer, others can relieve our pain. Sympathy, therefore, arises out of that very first close relationship we experience as a baby with a nurse. Early human experiences always link pain and pleasure to the presence or absence of another person. The first thing we learn is not how to look after ourselves but, rather, how to be dependent on one another. While Smith notes the infant's dependence on others in his epistemology (published in his posthumous *Essays on Philosophical Subjects*), this is not emphasized in his moral psychology. Rather, the first step toward the recognition of one's moral responsibilities is the experience of being judged by others in play or at school.

There are two ways to read this difference between Smith and Grouchy. The first is to see it as a progression rather than a departure. Smith and Grouchy both emphasize the role(s) interactions with others play in the development of the relevant dispositions and skills of morality, but Smith has left out dependency, which

---

3. For background, see Ryan Patrick Hanley, "Adam Smith and Virtue," in *The Oxford Handbook of Adam Smith*, ed. C. Berry, C. Smith, and M. P. Paganelli (Oxford: Oxford University Press, 2013), 230–232; and Eric Schliesser, "Counterfactual Causal Reasoning in Smithian Sympathy," *Revue internationale de philosophie* 3 (2014): 307–316.

Grouchy considers a fundamental form of intersubjectivity. This is not an accident. While Smith has quite a bit to say about child development in his account of the senses and the development of language faculty, Smith paradigmatically treats social life as an exchange of needs and wants among approximate equals. That is, he associates dependency with feudal hierarchy. From Grouchy's perspective, Smith ignores the original dependency of infants on others.[4] Another possible reading suggests that Grouchy is intuiting theories about human development and psychology that were not discussed until very recently, but that Smith, understandably, is not. This would be the concept of shared attention and the theory that infant development is tied to this capacity to communicate the object of one's needs to another human being.[5]

There are three further important disagreements between Smith and Grouchy. First, as noted earlier, for Grouchy, fellow-feeling with the suffering of others is central to her account of sympathy. We are motivated to relieve the misery of others because it makes us feel better to see their distress removed. Smith associates versions of such a view with the selfish hypothesis of Mandeville, Hobbes, and Rousseau, but it is fundamentally a naturalization, even a secularization of Christian charity. For Smith, fellow-feeling—often the outcome of a sympathetic process—is always pleasing; the desire for this (second-order) feeling is itself action guiding. This means that for Smith, we are driven in social life primarily to a certain kind of

---

4. This difference between Grouchy and Smith seems to anticipate, as Karin Brown noted in the introduction to the critical edition of Sophie de Grouchy, *Letters on Sympathy* (ed. Karin Brown, trans. James Edwards McClellan III, Transactions of the American Philosophical Society 98 [Philadelphia, PA: American Philosophical Society, 2008]), the arguments of care theorists who point out that the liberal values of independence fail to take into account the fact that no human being is independent throughout his or her life, and that we all require someone to care for us at some point or other.

5. We thank Mary Ellen Waithe and Heidi Maibom for suggestions that have improved his paragraph.

companionship and mutual accommodation, and without the mediation of language, are less prone to charity.

Second, we have noted that Grouchy is silent on the impartial spectator. But Grouchy also makes no place for, and completely ignores, one of the other central concepts in Smith's moral psychology: propriety. Judgments of propriety fundamentally are judgments of aptness about another's intentions, given the circumstances of a situation. This gives Smith's moral theory, when it comes to individual morality, a strongly deontic or even situationist flavor. For Smith, moral judgments are really about judgments of particular characters in particular circumstances. Because she bypasses propriety altogether, these features are absent in Grouchy's moral theory.

This is connected to a third difference. For Grouchy, a properly developed human being, who lives in a society that does not actively discourage sympathy—that is, with good laws and institutions and no excessive inequality—will feel sympathy for anyone who suffers. This is because, on her account, one learns to feel for humanity in general; this she associates with reason. For her, fellow-feeling with suffering is constitutive of the feeling of humanity, but it requires reflection and abstraction to become a true moral feeling. The full feeling of humanity—universal sympathy, which originates in a relation of dependency—is a social and intellectual achievement that we can all act on.

In Smith's writings, humanity is also an important principle of morality that transcends principles of justice and equity. But he treats it as a "soft power" (*TMS* III.3.4) and "soft virtue" (*TMS* III.3.37); that is, he thinks the feeling of humanity is motivationally weak. For him, we primarily sympathize with particular individuals, not with abstractions (this is very clear in Smith's criticism of Hume's moral theory). So, for Smith, the "dictates" of humanity can be proper norms of judgment, but they are rarely action guiding. This is probably the case because, from Smith's perspective, humanity is associated with intellectual achievement and is too refined a thought. While Grouchy and Smith both advocate for public enlightenment, Grouchy is de facto more optimistic about its full possibility, once society's institutions have been properly reformed, than is Smith.

2.4 OTHER WRITINGS

Although we are not aware of existing manuscripts by Grouchy—indeed, even the manuscript of the *Letters* is lost, so that we had to work with the first edition—it seems that she did write more. In her testament, she left papers pertaining to financial matters and to Condorcet's oeuvre to her daughter, Eliza Condorcet O'Connor. But she left other papers—which we have not been able to trace—to her sister, Charlotte Cabanis. It is possible that among these papers were other manuscripts in Sophie's hand. We know that in 1792, she had started to draft a novel, but she didn't think it would be very good, as she wrote to Etienne Dumont:

> As to the other mess, it contains as yet only a few weak traces of a development of character and passions, and that is not yet strengthened by any of the circumstances that make a novel interesting. One of the main causes of my laziness when it comes to working on it is (1) difficulty in obtaining good advice (will some arrive from overseas!), (2) the fear of not having the means of executing the ideas which, in other hands could enrich the subject matter, but in mine, will probably make it less.

This was the same letter in which she had asked Dumont to comment on the draft of the *Letters*. Dumont did not, apparently, offer any feedback, but as this did not stop her from working on the *Letters*, we might presume that she also continued work on the novel—or was she discouraged by what she saw as the lack of spark? Other pieces of writing that we know of only second hand are her translations. According to her aunt, while she was at convent school, Sophie translated Tasso's *Jerusalem* and an unnamed work by Arthur Young.[6] We suspect that she translated a work by Paine.[7] Thomas Paine could speak and write French, but didn't like to, and during his collaboration with the Condorcets on *Le Républicain*, his work had to be translated before it could be printed. We know of one piece that Dumont—who was a professional translator, at the time working with Jeremy Bentham—refused to translate. He did not like Paine, and moreover, for some obscure reason, Paine had agreed to let the young Achilles Duchatelet print the piece as his own.[8] Dumont wanted nothing to do with that, so they would have had to find another translator—and that, we suspect, would have been Grouchy,

6. Probably his *Tour in Ireland* or "Farmer's Letter to the People of England." He became more famous in France when he visited the country in 1787, but the translation was done in 1785. "La chanoiness, ecrivait Mme Dupaty au President, exerce toujours tous ses talents, en depit du mal aux yeux. Elle traduit, seule, du Tasse et le sublime Young." A. Guillois, *La Marquise de Condorcet, Sa Famille, Son Salon, Ses Amis 1764-1822* (Paris: Paul Ollendorff, 1897), 33. The reference to La Tasse is probably to Tasso's *Liberation of Jerusalem*, (2009) in which case she would have been translating also from the Italian.

7. Paine's letter was originally written in English and translated for the first volume of *Le Republicain* (7–11). The English version can be found in *The Political Writings of Thomas Paine* (New York: Solomon King, 1830), 2:263–266.

8. "Avis aux Français," *Le Republicain* 1:5, Condorcet and Paine 1991. This article was previously published as a placard and in Brissot's paper *Le Patriote Français*, July 2, 1791. It was signed "Duchatelet," but—as we know through Dumont—written by Paine and translated by Grouchy. Duchatelet first approached Dumont, who refused on the grounds that it was foolhardy to advertise oneself as a republican without the backing of the government and that it was not a good idea for Duchatelet to sign his own name to a text written by Paine (one also suspects that Dumont, even then, was not fond of Paine, he describes the enterprise as one between "an American and a young fool from the French aristocracy who put themselves forward to change the face of France") See Etienne Dumont, *Souvenirs sur Mirabeau et sur les deux premieres Assemblées Législatives* (Paris: Librairie de Charles Gosselin, 1832), 321–322.

the only member of the group involved in *Le Républicain* apart from Dumont, who was skilled in translation.[9] But her involvement in *Le Républicain* did not stop at translating Paine's work. It is highly likely that two pieces in that very short-lived publication (it lasted only the summer of 1791) were penned by Grouchy. One, "A Letter from a Young Mechanic," is likely entirely her own. The other, a reflection on the king's memoir, is probably a collaboration with Dumont, or at least a revision of Dumont's work.

Dumont writes in his memoir that he had begun to draft a piece for *Le Républicain*, and he left the draft at the Condorcet's home before leaving for England. He was surprised, he says, to find the piece published in two issues of the journal with many changes he did not recognize or approve of, mostly because of their anti-royalist sentiment. The journal had been founded when the king tried to leave France. At the time, Dumont, like Condorcet, Paine, and Duchatellet, thought a republic was the solution to France's problems. But later, with the return of the king, Dumont changed his mind and decided that France should settle for a constitutional monarchy. The piece, which is long and was printed across two issues of the paper, is certainly not in favor of a constitutional monarchy, but it is fiercely republican, thus corresponding to Dumont's and others' description of Grouchy's propensities.

Condorcet, in a letter addressed to his daughter in the weeks before his death, wrote that Grouchy had written other fragments on moral and political philosophy, which she should read in order to educate herself.[10] These fragments may well be among the lost papers. Did they eventually become more than fragments? Or, were they perhaps incorporated into the already existing draft of the eight *Letters*

---

9. Nicolas de Condorcet and Thomas Paine, *Aux Origines de la Republique 1789-1792*, Vol. 3: *Le Républicain par Condorcet et Thomas Paine, 1791* (Paris: EDHIS, 1991).

10. Lukes and Urbinani, *Condorcet: Political Writings*, 204.

on Sympathy? All these options are possible. It is also possible that after her husband's death, Grouchy set aside her own writing in order to work on the more lucrative translation of Smith (as she needed the money), and then on the all-consuming project of editing her husband's complete works. But even the editing work was not without some creative philosophical input from her, at least at the beginning.

In 1794, when Condorcet fled his hiding place in Paris, he left a manuscript of an introduction to an encyclopedic project he would never complete. This manuscript was published a few months after his death, edited by Grouchy. The published book, *The Sketch of Human Progress*, does not entirely correspond to the manuscript, with a total of forty added passages, a third of which are at least a paragraph long, and over 1500 smaller corrections.[11] These differences prompted a later editor of Condorcet's work, the academician François Arago, to ignore this first edition, "full of mistakes" as he saw it, and to go back to Condorcet's own words, in the manuscript he left his wife. This was, of course, in complete disregard of the fact that husband and wife had worked closely together throughout their marriage, but especially in the last months of Condorcet's life. It was, in fact, Grouchy who prompted Condorcet to start work on the *Sketch.* And if she did make changes or additions, these may well have been either her own legitimate contributions as a co-writer or ideas she and Condorcet had discussed but he had not had time to add to the text. By writing off her edition as a mistake, Arago erased Grouchy's contribution to this influential work.[12]

---

11. These are catalogued in Jean-Pierre Schandeler and Pierre Crépel, eds., *Notes sur le Tableau Historique des progrès de l'esprit humain, projets, Esquisse, Fragments et Notes (1772-1794)* (Paris: Institut National D'Etudes Démographiques, 2004).

12. For a discussion of this, see Sandrine Bergès, "Family, Gender and Progress: Sophie de Grouchy and Her Exclusion in the Publication of Condorcet's *Sketch of Human Progress,*" *Journal of the History of Ideas* 70, no. 2 (2018): 267–283.

A few months later, the government, wanting to atone for the death and persecution of Condorcet, commissioned an edition of the philosopher's last work, written in hiding. Sophie put together the text from notes she had worked on with Condorcet, and it was published in 1795. It was translated into English (perhaps by Grouchy?) almost immediately, and read and annotated by John Adams.[13]

---

13. See Zoltán Haraszti, "John Adams Flays a Philosophe: Annotations on Condorcet's Progress of the Human Mind," *William and Mary Quarterly* 7, no. 2 (1950): 223–254.

Chapter 3

Selected Themes

In this chapter, we call attention to some important themes in the *Letters* in addition to those discussed in sections 1.3 and 2.2–2.3. We do not intend to be exhaustive; we have focused on those themes we consider most fruitful for students coming to Grouchy for the first time.

3.1 POLITICAL PHILOSOPHY: REPUBLICANISM

Reading the *Letters* as a republican text situates them within a larger historico-philosophical context, one that is currently being recovered for that period. This does not just make sense because other writers of the same period are being read as republicans (Mary Wollstonecraft, for instance, who until recently was thought of as a liberal thinker, is now seen by many as an important source for feminist republicanism).[1] It also places Grouchy in a republican context, highlighting the importance of her thought for the French Revolution and vice versa. Few political philosophers write in a vacuum; most are influenced

---

1. See, especially Lena Halldenius, *Mary Wollstonecraft and Feminist Republicanism* (London: Routledge, 2015); and chs. 7–11 in Sandrine Bergès and Alan Coffee, *The Social and Political Philosophy of Mary Wollstonecraft* (Oxford: Oxford University Press, 2016).

by or wish to influence the events unfolding around them. But when the events are as remarkable as a revolution, then it makes no sense to ignore their impact on the work we are looking at. In the case of Grouchy, it is even clearer that she wished to participate, through her writings, in the making of the new Republic; in the summer of 1791, together with Condorcet and a few friends, she established a political journal, *Le Républicain*, the purpose of which was to enlighten the public as to what republicanism was.

Le Républicain lasted for just over a month. It was begun after Louis XVI attempted to leave France, seeking help from foreign powers against the Revolution. It ended with the king's return and the incident of the Champ de Mars (the 'Champ de Mars Massacre), when the army, led by the Condorcets' old friend, Lafayette, turned against the demonstrating crowds. The aim of *Le Républicain* stated in its opening article, "Avis aux Français," was to promote the ideal of republicanism, attempting to make it more respectable and better understood than it was at the time: "to enlighten minds on the subject of republicanism, which is slandered because it is misunderstood."[2]

A theme that is strongly present in the articles of *Le Républicain* is that of the threat to freedom constituted by monarchy. It does not matter, says Paine, whether a monarch is "a fool a hypocrite or a tyrant"—what matters is that this individual has "absolute power" over everyone, including those who are not yet born.[3] Condorcet takes this further in his letter to foreign powers—the article after Paine's—in which he says that unless there is equality, some may be tempted to introduce oppression of the many by the few. Perhaps so as not to unduly offend foreigners who may support monarchy in

2. "Avis aux Français," *Le Républicain* 1: 5. This article was previously published as a placard and in Brissot's paper *Le Patriote Francais*, on July 2, 1791.
3. *Le Republicain* 1:5 Condorcet and Paine, 1991.

their own countries, Condorcet is at pains to highlight the corrupting and harmful effects of monarchy as a *potential*, rather than an actuality. In other words, not all monarchs are necessarily intent on harming their subjects, but their position of absolute authority means that should they wish to do so, they could. So, whereas Condorcet recognizes that revolution may not be desirable for all the neighboring states at the same time as the French are revolting, he is very clear that living under a monarch is at all times a form of slavery and that people interested in liberty will at some point need to overthrow that monarchy.

This emphasis on the potential and arbitrary character of monarchical oppression puts the writers of *Le Républicain* squarely in the neo-republican tradition—that is, emphasizing the idea that liberty is freedom from domination. It also puts them in direct opposition to those *philosophes*, like Voltaire, who favored enlightened despotism. To be free is not, in that sense, merely to be free of interference—as the subject of a benign monarch might be—but also to be free of the potential interference of one who has absolute power over us and may choose to exert that power at any point in time. The benign monarch will die, and his heir—who will rule over the next generation—may not be benign or enlightened. And, as Paine and Condorcet both point out, it is not the case that a people who know their children might not be free can call themselves free.

According to Condorcet, "The word 'revolutionary' applies only to those revolutions whose purpose is freedom."[4] That is, what is overthrown in a revolution is any individual or institution that constitutes tyranny of the people. According to Condorcet, as well as Grouchy, and indeed according to that other republican philosopher of the period, Mary Wollstonecraft, tyranny is the arbitrary domination of citizens by their ruler or the institutions. The idea

4. Condorcet, *On Revolution*, in Lukes and Urbinati, *Condorcet: Political Writings*, 190.

that a potential domination is a threat to liberty is also developed in Grouchy's *Letters on Sympathy*. While she is relatively silent about sketching the constitutional arrangements, she is very interested in exploring the effects of important institutions (law, education, economy, child-rearing, etc.).

In the previous paragraph we write "relatively silent" for two reasons: first, Grouchy is clearly adamant that feudal institutions, which secure legal and tax privileges and excemptions for royalty, the aristocracy, and the clergy, should be abolished. Second, Grouchy does offer one positive and rather democratic proposal in Letter VII: all government "appointments" should be the product of a free election or consensus choice. Unfortunately, she does not offer more details on what she has in mind. But if taken literally, and we see no reason not to do so, she advocates thoroughgoing democratic accountability of all government officials.

When it comes to the principles of institutional design, she is more elaborate. In particular, Grouchy hopes that these will be of assistance in the creation of the new republic. As well as getting human relations right, and making sure that her account of the role of sympathy traces back to physiological principles, Grouchy wants to show the possibility of rebuilding human relations in a world where tyranny and arbitrary power are no longer directly present, but have left harmful traces in the form of laws, institutions, traditions, and attitudes of one class toward another. Thus, the *Letters* are also an attempt at stating the ethical theory behind the sort of republicanism defended by Grouchy and Condorcet in showing how arbitrary domination prevents people from developing sympathy toward each other, and therefore keeps them from developing moral judgment and mutual respect.

From a modern perspective, what is most notable is that Grouchy believes social institutions can be so designed that if they function properly and impartially, then incentives are properly aligned, and these institutions can help cultivate and develop virtue and moral judgment in citizens, as well as mutual respect. Rather than preaching (secular) virtue to the citizens from the top down, these institutions will facilitate the development of the "disposition most favorable to virtue" (Letter I), as it were, from the bottom up. As she puts it in Letter VII, "laws . . . ought to supplement citizens' conscience," rather than being, as they are "all too often," oppressive "chains instead." In so doing, they can contribute to the perfection of human nature.

There are several obvious signs that Grouchy is a republican, in the sense that she is defending a view of freedom as nondomination. First, she makes it clear that what is wrong with prerevolutionary France, and any monarchy, is not that the monarch is or was a tyrant but, rather, that he could be. In other words, the people have no choice but to be ruled by the person who inherits the throne, whatever qualities as a ruler that person has; and this, republicans claim, is a threat to liberty that should not be tolerated: "As if reason could approve of leaving a sovereign (who may be a tyrant) unchecked except by his remorse, the progress of the enlightenment, or the despair of his victims?" (Letter VI).

How does sympathy help with this? Domination, according to Grouchy, affects human relationships such that people who have been used to look upon each other as dominator and dominated will find it difficult to look upon each other as equals. In Letter VII, Grouchy gives an example of such a problematic relationship between a rich employer and his worker. Neither sees the other as fully human, so the one can tyrannize and the other has no compunction about stealing. Making sure that sympathy is well developed in all, she says, is the only way to ensure that freedom acquired through the revolution applies to social relations.

3.2 LEGAL PHILOSOPHY AND POLITICAL ECONOMY

In Letter VIII, Grouchy announces that her legal philosophy is ameliorative: she argues against existing "abuses" and she reiterates what a "small number of philosophers have been saying over the last few years." With these modern reformers, she argues, the European nations who prided themselves on being civilized were actually marked by barbarous laws. While it is undeniable that her legal philosophy brings together a number of themes from Hume, Smith, and, especially, Beccaria, her self-presentation understates some of her originality and distinctiveness, which is easy to miss given the terseness at points where she is most distinctive. To modern readers, her legal philosophy blends at times into political theory and political economy; in his section, we explain why this is so.

For Grouchy, the law serves a number of purposes. The primary one—and here, she decisively sides with the then-modern reformers inspired by Beccaria—is to deter crimes (Letter VIII). She treats criminals, juries, and judges as responding to incentives *and* as evaluators of the fairness of particular laws. Incentives and such judgments of fairness interact and have predictable effects.[5]

So, for example, the law deters not by its severity but by its predictable and regular enforcements, as well as its perceived fairness. Very harsh laws—and in the eighteenth century, theft could be a capital crime—that are thought disproportional to the crime are also badly enforced, thereby undermining the authority and effectiveness of the laws as deterrence.[6] It is not entirely clear if she thinks that such

---

5. Grouchy presupposes that the dispositions of human nature are despite variance fairly predictable in responding to incentives.

6. On the significance of judgments of proportionality in Hume's and Smith's social philosophy, see Eric Schliesser, *Adam Smith: Systematic Philosopher and Public Thinker* (Oxford: Oxford University Press, 2017), 115–118

judgments of proportionality are context sensitive or invariant, but she does think such judgments *ought* to be informed by "justice and reason." She implies, however, that in practice it is local and religious prejudices that inform, without fully determining, such judgments of proportionality.[7]

There are a number of important points lurking here. On Grouchy's view, which she shares with Hume, Smith, and Madison, the *authority* of the law can be traced to, and rests on, the good opinion of those who are meant to enforce it and whose lives are regulated by it. This means it must be intelligible to the "average reason" of ordinary citizens (Letter VIII).[8]

The opinions of citizens will be shaped by the institutions of society—including the law—so there is something self-reinforcing about this authority. As we have seen in section 3.2, the law's ability to shape citizens' consciences is, in addition to deterrence, one of its important social functions. But Grouchy is also clear that bad laws become self-undermining when they provoke a critical reaction, informed by "ordinary conscience" against them (Letter VIII).

Laws that favor the rich or make exceptions for feudal and clerical privilege are, in their partiality, straightforwardly self-undermining. So are punishments that appear to be arbitrary—say, owing to judicial discretion—that allow favoritism and bias. In addition, a system of laws can undermine the authority of the law when some such laws prove to be empty (because they are unenforceable or whose violations are difficult to prove) or unequally enforced. These laws are felt to violate "natural rights." When such laws do so, they undermine

---

7. Proportionality is central to her treatment of the sympathetic mechanism: "we feel sympathy for physical pains and pleasures in proportion to our understanding of their strengths and consequences, such as we have gained by experiencing them ourselves; in the same way, we are in general more sympathetic toward those moral pains and pleasures we are likely to experience" (Letter IV).

8. The idea goes back to Plato's *Laws*, but it is absent in Beccaria.

not just their own authority but also their role in shaping public conscience and "mutual respect."

Laws that violate public conscience also generate anger and hatred. Echoing a long line of thinkers, including Machiavelli and Spinoza, Grouchy notes that the existence of such "outrage" is a clear epistemic signal that something is amiss. Such anger is evidence of "a vicious system of legislation" that reflects how interests are set against each other (Letter IV). Good legislation prevents this mutual anger and brings "together the interests of individuals," such that mutual respect becomes possible. Grouchy does not go so far as Rousseau in introducing a general will, but she does think that interests can be harmonized in a proper institutional framework.

A subtler problem occurs with laws that actually encourage worse crimes than they purport to punish (and prevent). So, for example, if a burglary and murder have the same punishment, then murders (which can eliminate potential witnesses) during robbery are actually incentivized because the criminals "have nothing to lose" (Letter VIII).[9] In addition, judges and juries grow less likely to convict those who commit minor offenses carrying harsh penalties. It is not clear that this undermines the authority of the law—because it is not entirely clear that the problem violates "ordinary conscience" or is noticed by "average reason"—but it does violate the main purpose of the law: rather than deterring crime, unpunished criminal actions are multiplied. A philosophical reformer of the law must, thus, take such wider consequences into account in proposing legal reforms.

Because prerevolutionary legal codes provided a whole range of tax privileges and exemptions to the aristocracy and clergy, and prevented the free movement of people and goods, it is natural for an eighteenth-century reader to see legal reform and free trade as possible instruments for generating more legal and financial equality.

---

9. We take the quote out of context, although the point is not.

Grouchy is explicit that financial and legal inequality create social distance, such that the classes become unable to "judge one another" fairly. This undermines the proper functioning of the law, because the judiciary and prerevolutionary *parlements* (provincial appellate courts) were drawn from the wealthier classes. In becoming more impartial, the law would create more economic equality and, thereby, favor the conditions of "mutual respect."

The idea that impartial law and free trade would be equalizing reflects the extreme financial and legal inequality that existed in eighteenth-century France. This was so, even though Grouchy assumes that what she calls "natural inequalities"—that is, differences in intelligence, effort, behavior patterns, and fertility[10]—causes unequal financial outcomes (Letter VII). She adds a thought experiment that suggests existing inequalities are "unnatural."

Thus far, we have left Grouchy's account of rights and property unexamined.[11] In Letter VI, she offers a neo-Lockean account of property originating in the (presumably) hypothetical "state of nature." There, "a man who, in the state of nature, has taken pains to cultivate a field, to supervise its harvest, has a right to this harvest." She avoids Locke's metaphysical claims and primarily relies on the thought that labor bestows a claim on that thing. The underlying idea seems to be that work and possession generate reasonable expectations (this echoes Smith's treatment). As Grouchy explains: "because by taking it away from him, making his work useless, depriving him of what he had long looked forward to, and of the possession he deserved, we

---

10. It is not entirely clear if she thinks that more children will lead to more or less wealth over time. For Hume and Smith, a growing population was an effect, not a cause, of growing wealth.

11. The remainder of this section draws on Eric Schliesser, "Sophie de Grouchy: The Tradition(s) of Two Liberties, and the Missing Mother(s) of Liberalism," in *Women and Liberty, 1600-1800: Philosophical Essays*, ed. Jacqueline Broad and Karen Detlefsen (Oxford: Oxford University Press, 2017), 109–122.

hurt him more than we would should we deprive him of a similar harvest that just happened to be within his reach."

What makes something a reasonable expectation is, of course, contestable (and corruptible). But the use of harvest in this example of explaining the (conceptual) origin and legitimacy of property rights is not accidental; harvests are always temporarily removed from much of the original work; they are anticipated because they require considerable planning and foresight. They involve delayed gratification ("he had long looked forward to"). In addition to the harm against the person, the social utility of such labor is undermined. That it has such social utility is a consequence of Grouchy's larger, physiocratic commitments (recall section 1.3 regarding Letter VII), which entail that agriculture is the source of social surplus. But she uses the point in an interesting fashion in the harvest example.

Before we get to it, it is useful to make an important distinction. The (individual) idea of justice as such is, for Grouchy, grounded in a particular kind of experience: "when we harm or benefit others, we experience sentiments that, together with reflection, give us the abstract idea of moral good and evil. From this idea we get that of justice and injustice. Individual ideas of justice are linked to the feeling of pleasure or pain when we benefit or harm others" (Letter VI).[12] Grouchy's position echoes Mandeville and Rousseau here.

But the whole scheme or system of justice—that is, strict property rights—is justified by an interesting argument Grouchy offers in light of her harvest example: "reason demands that we give him preference even when he does not need all of his harvest while another has a real need of some—and this is precisely what constitutes right. It is grounded in reason, on the necessity of general laws to rule over actions, common to all men, and dispenses us from examining the

---

12. A terminological point: "reflection" should not be confused with reason. In Lockean psychology it is the part of the mind where mental abstraction takes place.

motives and consequences of each particular act." Not unlike Hume's defense of the systemic rule of law, she rejects what we may call the episodic or act-consequentialist justification of individual need.

But the appeal to reason here is grounded, first, in a general principle ("the necessity of general laws to rule over actions") and, second, in a good consequence (the legal system can avoid judging "the motives and consequences of each particular act"). For it is simpler and politically less dangerous to have a regime that evaluates actions through a law-like rule than one that encourages us to look into the unique "motives and consequences of each particular act." People's inner thoughts are not easily available, after all. The generalized rule (property rights) also facilitates a species of equality in which everybody is treated equally under the law. While not unlike Smith, Grouchy fails to note that some disabled are unable to work—the rule applies to all those capable of working. It is, thus, an egalitarian principle; Grouchy calls it a "natural equality." The general right to property protects one, in part, from the individual claims based on need by others.

It follows from Grouchy's position, again not unlike Adam Smith's, that established and inherited claims to property not founded on work are treated with suspicion. She calls such claims "prerogative" and associates them with the "so-called rights of the despot, the noble, and the priest." Such prerogatives that present themselves as a right merely "hide and disguise the power of might."

3.3 AESTHETICS

Aesthetics—and in particular, the effects of beauty—is of central importance to the argument of the *Letters*. Grouchy brackets the metaphysical question about the nature and origin of beauty. Rather, she settles for a pragmatic definition: something is beautiful if it gives us pleasure to watch (or hear, etc.) it. This means it is grounded in sensibility (recall section 2.3). And this means that, for her, paying attention to beauty and beautiful people can be a significant source of "happiness" (Letter III), especially if we sympathize with them.

The significance of this is highlighted in Letter IV, where she takes on the political problem of demagoguery, which, as she experienced, is very dangerous to republican and democratic forms of government. According to Grouchy, we are naturally partial to, and even obsessively interested in, beautiful people. This is not all bad because we enjoy thinking about beauty and, so, our directed interest in it has epistemic payoffs. It makes us more accurate in noticing features of the beautiful: "we enjoy thinking about him, and the interest we feel intensifies our observations, and increases their accuracy" (Letter III). Our attraction to others can be a solid basis of friendship, even love. But Grouchy warns that such partiality toward the beautiful can also be a source of bias, even pernicious bias, in the context of political life.

For, according to Grouchy's moral psychology, we do not merely want to admire beautiful people from, as it were, afar but, due to the effects of sympathy, we also want to actively contribute to *their* happiness. Rhetorically skillful demagogues, who have a "manipulative art," take advantage of this in two ways. First, their words and speeches seduce us by their beauty and flattery. Demagogues ignore objections and facts that may be discordant. So, they present themselves with conviction, and this can be attractive, especially to people who are insecure about their own opinions. It is especially appealing when they flatter the audience and boldly make their prejudices seem natural. This makes the targeted audience feel special, even beautiful, in turn.

Second, demagogues present themselves in spectacular environments with large crowds, which themselves become a source of beauty, and by their sympathetic co-attention to the demagogue, sway ours: "the attention of the crowd commands ours, and its eager-ness, forewarning our sensibility of the emotions it is about to experi-ence, sets them in motion." So, demagogues use beauty and sympathy to enhance their impact. The cumulate effect of demagoguery is, thus, that people want to aid a demagogue in his or her endeavors, even if it is not in their own interest as properly understood.

Aesthetics is also taken on directly by Grouchy in her treatment of the problem of tragedy—a topic widely discussed in eighteenth-century thought. A simplified version of this topic is as follows: Why do viewers find pleasure, or something like pleasure, in the dramatic representation of an action that is painful and repellent in real life?[13] This generated a huge amount of reflection in the mid-eighteenth century. As Grouchy notes in Letter IV, Adam Smith had also taken it on in *TMS*. Modern audiences may encounter a version of this ques-tion when they enjoy a horror movie.[14]

The problem of tragedy is an especially acute one for Grouchy, for two related reasons. First, given her account of sympathy, we do not find the suffering of others pleasant, and we try to remove it. But while audiences sometimes leave a theater in disgust (or avoid going to a horror movie), we generally do not try to help those suffering on stage. So, why do we willingly go to watch tragedies and enjoy them? Second, she claims (and here she adapts a view standard since the Renaissance)[15] that the "point of tragedy" is in part ethical: it is in "great part to make our sympathy for the misfortunes of others seem pleasant." So, tragedy serves a didactic purpose in virtue of being pleasing; but given her account of sympathy, why would we go to see a tragedy and expect to enjoy it?

13. See Earl R. Wasserman, "The Pleasures of Tragedy," *ELH* 14, no. 4 (1947): 283. We thank James Harris for calling our attention to Wasserman.
14. On this, see Noel Carroll, "The Nature of Horror," *Journal of Aesthetics and Art Criticism* 46, no.1 (1987): 51–59
15. Wasserman, "Pleasures of Tragedy," 284.

It is central to Grouchy's argument that we sympathize more with pain that we are *likely* to experience (Letter IV). This is as true for physical as for psychological discomfort, even if, according to her, we tend to sympathize more with physical suffering than with psychological suffering.

So, her strategy in considering the problem of tragedy is to emphasize two features of a tragic performance. First, the events portrayed are unlikely to happen to the viewers. Most of us are not kings or heroes, and so according to Grouchy we really do not identify directly with the protagonists and so do not really sympathize with them.[16] Second, tragedies prepare our sensibility slowly and avoid "suddenly confronting" us "with the heartbreaking sight of physical pain." So, de facto, these two features imply that we actually sympathize very little or very lightly with the agents portrayed. The exceptions—pity for the fallen mighty—prove the rule: "if we have more compassion for their misfortunes than for those of others, it is only because kings who seem to have been preserved from misfortune by their elevation strike us as more sensitive to them" (Letter IV).

As a solution to the problem of tragedy, this is not satisfying. And because she rejects Smith's idea that the outcome of the sympathetic process is always pleasing, she seems in a bad position to offer any such solution. But she is clearly assuming some background commitments that mitigate the issues with her position. For example, when she introduces the problem of tragedy, she discusses the nature of boredom, which we do anything to avoid. It is so "unbearable" that "we do not fear to give ourselves over to painful sensations, and it is the desire to avoid boredom that leads us to seek the proximity of the idea of suffering" (Letter II). This means that we subject ourselves to tragedy in order to avoid a worse fate

16. This may be true in classical tragedy, but is less so in, say, modern horror movies.

(boredom), especially if the ideas encountered in it are fairly novel. (This is why it matters to Grouchy that in tragedy we encounter events we are unlikely to experience ordinarily.) These ideas had been used by two influential and widely read French theorists, Dubos and Fontenelle, in addressing the problem of tragedy.[17] (It would be a surprise if she had not encountered either in her education and readings.)

Grouchy adds an important consideration. We can identify with the victims of tyranny in a tragedy because we can be subject to the same tyrant. In Letter II, she makes the point by evoking Sophocles's *Antigone*. But we do not find this pleasant or attractive at all. Rather, this identification activates self-pity, and so we find the actions of the tragedy of interest (even if unpleasant). This serves the didactic purpose of generating an interest in humanity. So, the other part of Grouchy's strategy in addressing the problem of tragedy is to simply deny one of its premises: we do not really enjoy a tragedy even when, especially, we find it of interest.[18]

By building on the mechanisms of sensibility and sympathy, Grouchy's *Letters* calls attention to the centrality of aesthetic experience in political and social life.[19] Despots, monarchs, and democracies all draw on aesthetic practices to guide our attention and actions, but the institutions of society also shape our aesthetic responses. That is, Grouchy calls attention to the significance of political and moral considerations within aesthetic experience. Once one recognizes this, it is no surprise that tragedy is so central to her argument: tragedy both represents these characteristics and is a means, sometimes obliquely, to reflect on them.

---

17. Wasserman, "Pleasures of Tragedy," 290–293.
18. Since Kant, there is a tendency to view aesthetics as special realm of disinterest. But this does not preclude taking interest in objects of aesthetic experience.
19. Spiros Tegos, "Sympathie morale et tragédie sociale: Sophie de Grouchy lectrice d'Adam Smith," *Noesis* 21 (2013): 265–292.

PART II

TRANSLATION

Letters to C***, on
The Theory of Moral Sentiments

Chapter 4

Letter I

It seems to me that man has no more interesting object of meditation than himself, my dear C***.[1] Is there, indeed, a more fulfilling
and pleasant way to pass the time than to turn one's soul onto itself,
study its operations, trace its movements; to employ our faculties to
observe and puzzle each other out and to seek out and understand
the fleeting and secret laws that guide our intelligence and our sensibility?[2] To be often in one's own company strikes me as the sweetest
and the wisest way of living; for it joins the pleasures of lively and
deep sentiments to those of wisdom and philosophy. It establishes
the soul in a state of well-being that is the first element of happiness,
and the disposition most favorable to virtue. Many never achieve the
distinction and happiness they are capable of because they are ignorant of this life, or they hold it in scorn or fear, which, perfecting reason and sensibility at the same time, improves us for our sake and that
of others.[3] You know what faith I place in this kind of life; and so, after

1. Although it has been suggested that C*** was Condorcet, the 1830 edition of the *Letters*
stated the full name as Cabanis, the Condorcets' good friend and Sophie's brother-in-law.
Their common interest in physiology, Cabanis's work on how physical constitution affects
morality, and their continued correspondence on the subject make him the obvious
addressee of the *Letters*.
2. I translate "sensibilité" as either "sensibility" or "sensitivity," as there is no obvious fit for one
or the other.
3. Perfectionism not only is central to the argument of the *Letters* but is also the central theme
of Condorcet's last piece of writing, which Grouchy edited after his death and perhaps

the works that treat of the grand means of ensuring the happiness of men in society, I put first those that bring us back to ourselves, and make us dwell inside our souls.

Until now, I had not read Adam Smith's *The Theory of Moral Sentiments*; I had heard that the French translation of this famous work was not a good one,[4] and I did not know enough English to read the original text.[5] At last I ventured to read it; but instead of following the ideas of this Edinburgh philosopher, I became caught up in my own. While reading his chapters on sympathy, I composed others on the same subject. I will lay them for you here, so that you may judge me. I won't say that you may judge us, as I am far from pretending to be on a level with Smith.

As you know the subject of the first chapters is sympathy. Smith contented himself with asserting its existence and expounding its principal effects; I regretted that he held back from investigating further, that he did not discover its first cause and show, at last, why sympathy is the property of every sensible being susceptible to reflection.[6] You will see how I had the impudence to make up for these omissions.[7]

helped him write, the *Esquisse d'un Tableau des Progres de l'Esprit Humain*. Schandeler, Jean-Pierre, and Pierre Crépel, eds. *Notes sur le Tableau Historique des progrès de l'esprit humain, projets, Esquisse, Fragments et Notes (1772-1794)*. (Paris: Institut National D'Etudes Démographiques, 2004).

4. *The Theory of Moral Sentiments* had been translated twice by Marc-Antoine Eidous (1764) and Abbé Blavet (1775). Smith had been involved with both translations and found them sorely wanting. See Faccarello and Steiner, "The Diffusion."

5. We know that Grouchy in fact had a very good command of English, and that she had translated Young's *Tour in Ireland* while at convent school in 1785 (see Guillois, *La Marquise de Condorcet*, 38).

6. "Reflection" here refers to a cognitive faculty whereby impressions are transformed. See John Locke, *An Essay Concerning Human Understanding* (Hammondsworth: Penguin Classics, 1998), II.6; and *TMS*, VII.3.3.6, p. 328.

7. See the introduction, this volume, for a comparison of the *Letters* and *TMS*.

Sympathy is the disposition we have to feel in a way similar to others.[8]

Before we examine the causes of the sort of sympathy we experience when faced with a moral suffering, we must consider what the causes are of the kind we experience when faced with physical suffering.[9]

Any physical pain causes in its recipient a composite sensation.

First, it produces a local pain in the part of the body that is directly acted on by the cause of the pain.

It also produces a painful impression in all our organs, an impression quite distinct from that local pain, and which always accompanies it but can persevere without it.

In order to understand how distinct that sensation is from the local pain, one need only observe one's feelings after that pain goes away. Often, then, we experience at once the pleasure caused by the ending of the local pain and a general feeling of discomfort. This feeling is sometimes very distressing and can even, if particular causes make it endure, become harder to bear than those local pains, which are brief yet more intense, because it principally affects the organs which are the most essential to life's functions and the faculties to which we owe our sensitivity and intelligence.

This general sensation is renewed whenever we remember our sufferings: it renders that memory painful, always, and more or less vivid.

It is necessary to observe that this impression, though susceptible no doubt to some variation, is nonetheless the same for many very different local pains, at least when these pains are somewhat analogous,

---

8. "Sympathy, though its meaning was perhaps, originally the same, may now, however, without much impropriety, be made use of to denote our fellow-feeling with any passion whatever" (*TMS* I.1.1.5, p. 13).

9. "Moral" here means pertaining to the mind in a broad sense—see glossary, this volume.

by either their intensity or their nature. But when this impression is different for two pains of an opposite kind—the fracture of a bone or an internal organ injury—a person who has experienced both may experience a similar impression while remembering them, if time has weakened his memory of them, or if he doesn't stop long enough for his imagination and memory to transmit the sensations to which are tied the difference between these impressions.[10]

In the same way that the memory of suffering reproduces in us the painful impression that all our organs felt at the time, of the local pain that it caused us to experience, we experience this painful impression when—if we are able to recognize the symptoms of pain—we see a sensible being suffer, or we know that he is suffering.

Indeed, as soon as the development of our faculties and the repeated experience of pain grant us the ability to think about it abstractly, the very idea of pain will suffice to renew in us the general impression it once made on our organs.

This effect of suffering, therefore, follows from the physical and the moral manifestation of pain alike.

By moral manifestation of suffering, we understand either the idea that our memories give us of it or that which we receive sight or knowledge of someone else's suffering.

Sympathy for physical pains, therefore, is caused by the fact that the sensation produced in us by physical pain is a composite one, part of which can be renewed at the very idea of pain.

We can see now how a child with enough intelligence to distinguish the symptoms of suffering will sympathize with the person who displays such symptoms, how the sight of pain can affect her to the point of making her cry out, and cause her to run away from it; how she may be more or less moved, depending on how well she is

---

10. Smith briefly touches on the role of memory in bringing about sympathy in *TMS* I.1.2.4, p. 18.

acquainted with the symptoms of suffering, and has more or less sensibility, imagination, and memory.

The reproduction of the general impression of suffering on our organs depends on sensitivity, and especially on imagination. For this impression is more vivid when our sensitivity is stronger, its reproduction requires less effort when the impression is more vivid, and our imagination is better able to receive and preserve all the ideas that can help reproduce it.

Not only is the general impression of suffering reproduced by the idea of it, but its local impression can also sometimes be renewed when the memory or the idea of the pain strikes us vividly. In this way, when a person on whom a violent surgery was performed recalls it in all its circumstances, he fancies he can feel some of the local pain that he experienced then. Or again, the sight of an injured person, might, as well as cause a painful general impression, lead a person whose imagination is strong or easily moved to think that he himself is experiencing a local pain in that part of the body affected by the injury, and sometimes also in the adjoining parts connected to the same nerves. I once knew a woman who, having read in a medical book a very detailed piece about the diseases of the lungs, had so frightened her imagination as to the multiple ways in which this vitally important organ could be harmed that she fancied herself subject to the pains symptomatic of congestion of the lungs, and would not be convinced otherwise. Such examples are not infrequent, especially among that class of individuals who, through weakness of character and idleness, lack the means of fighting off the aberrations of their too active imaginations.[11]

---

11. On this topic, see *TMS* VI.2.3.19, p. 289. Unlike in modern usage, where the imagination is never truth-apt, in eighteenth-century terminology, the imagination can present truthful images of reality, but need not.

It is not hard to see that the general impression produced by the sight of physical pain is more easily renewed when we witness sufferings that we have been subject to, because in that case both our memories and the sight of their object arouse it in us. It is for this reason that the school of pain and adversity is so efficacious in rendering men more compassionate and humane. How great your need for this school, you rich and powerful, whose wealth, egoism, and customary power are an insuperable barrier between you and the very idea of misery and pain![12]

Elderly people, whose ability to feel is dulled, find it harder to experience the motions of sympathy for physical pain: if some do seem to be easily moved and often tearful, it is not the result of a strong sympathy but, instead, of the weakening of their organs, which doubles the power of pain on them. Therefore its very sight is a danger to them and may curtail their lives still.

One may ask why surgeons, doctors, and all those who care for the suffering are ordinarily less affected by the sight of pain than others. How, for instance, do surgeons find the nerve to probe a wound, brand and cauterize it, go deep inside delicate organs, through bloody and torn flesh, without the sight and sounds of agony affecting their own organs so that their hand will not shake, their sight not blur, nor their attention and judgment waver? Reflection will show that the main reason for this is not that the necessity of avoiding this pain— which would become unbearable if too often repeated—has hardened them against the impression of suffering (a rare insensitivity, and fortunately one that the heart can only contract through long and painful efforts). Instead, a habit of considering pain in relation to the preservation of the sufferer halts the impression of pain on them, and the idea of preventing a patient's destruction softens the often awful

12. This comment introduces the political significance of a society in which compassion is possible.

aspect of the affliction in the surgeon's eyes and the sharp cries of the plaints and agonies in his ears. This touching and pressing interest in saving the life of another, the attentiveness needed for finding the means to it, suspends, for his own preservation, the impression he receives from suffering. And benevolent nature preserves him from the impression of suffering whenever it would otherwise prevent him from being useful.[13]

It seems clear that the more we exercise our sensitivity, the stronger it becomes, unless by overexercising it we bring it to a degree which makes it wearying and painful and forces us to seek deliverance from it. When it is not exercised, sensitivity tends to weaken, and can only be moved by very strong impressions:

> The soul is a fire that must be fed
> *And which will die if it does not grow.*

—Voltaire[14]

How important it must be, therefore, to exercise children's sensitivity to the point where it will continue to develop as much as it is capable of—so that it can no longer be dulled by those things in life that tend to lead sensitivity astray.[15] These things lead us far from nature and ourselves by focusing our sensitivity on vain and selfish passions, leading us away from simple tastes, and from those natural leanings

13. This could be a direct praise of Cabanis, a physician himself, who although he seems not to have practiced much at all, overcame his sensibility to be useful to his friend, Condorcet, by procuring him the poison ring with which he may have committed suicide.
14. "Stances Irregulieres. A son Altesse Royale la princesse de Suede" (1747), in Voltaire, *Oeuvres Completes* (Paris: Garnier Frères, 1877–1885), t.8 587–588.
15. Here, Grouchy begins a discussion of the social importance of an education, which emphasizes the development of faculties that make compassion possible. Many of her arguments are close to Rousseau's, but her emphasis on the role of scientific education as a means to develop one's faculties is distinct and is closer to the philosophy of Adam Smith and Wollstonecraft.

in which the happiness of each person resides, the kind of happiness that does not require the sacrifice of others and that benefits all. Fathers, mothers, teachers—you nearly have in your hands the destiny of the next generation! How guilty you are if you allow your children to abort these precious germs of sensitivity which require, for their development, nothing more than the sight of suffering, the example of compassion, the tears of gratefulness, and an enlightened hand leading and moving them! How guilty you are if you care more about your children's success than about their virtue, if you are more impatient to see them gain popularity in their circle than to see their heart brim with indignation for an injustice, their faces turn pale at the sight of suffering, their hearts treat all men as brothers! Think less of their charms, their accomplishments, their employment; make their souls come forth with all the sentiments that nature has placed in them; teach them to be easily remorseful, delicately proud, and honest; let them not see suffering without being tormented by the need to bring relief. No less is needed in the midst of these oppressive barriers, raised between man and man from need, strength, and vanity, but that they should fear at each step to hurt rights or to neglect to repair some ancient wrong![16] That the sweet habit of doing good should teach them that it is through the heart that they will find happiness, and not through titles, luxury, dignities, or riches!

You have taught me that much, respectable mother, whose steps I so often followed under the decaying roof of the unfortunate, fighting destitution and suffering![17] I owe you my lifelong gratitude for

16. The idea that hereditary power always begins with injustice is a theme that runs through the *Letters*.
17. On Madame de Grouchy's character, see Guillois, *La Marquise de Condorcet*, p. 6; on her charity, p. 21. Note that here Grouchy differs greatly from Rousseau, for whom the place of the mother in a child's education is limited to lactation (and even then only if the mother has sufficiently good habits that she will not influence the child negatively, in which case a wet nurse is recommended; see the introduction to Rousseau, Jean-Jacques. *Emile: Or on Education*. Translated by Barbara Foxley. Everyman Classics. London. 1991.

every time I do good, and every time I feel the happy inspiration and sweet joy of doing so. Yes, seeing your hands relieve both misery and illness, and the suffering eyes of the unfortunate turning to you, softening as they blessed you, I felt my heart become whole, and the true good of social life was made clear to me, and appeared to me in the happiness of loving and serving humanity.

Because we receive pleasurable impressions through the same organs as we do painful ones, these impressions are subject to the same laws. All physical pleasure, as all physical pain, produces in us a sensation composed of a particular sensation of pleasure in the organ that receives it immediately, and a general sensation of well-being. And the latter can be renewed at the sight of pleasure, as a painful one can at the sight of pain.

We are, therefore, susceptible to feeling sympathy for physical pleasures that others experience, just as we are for their pains. Only, this sympathy is harder to provoke, and hence rarer: First, because the intensity of pleasure being lesser than that of pain, its general impression on our organs is harder to arouse. Second, because nearly all physical pleasures are by nature exclusive, giving us the idea and sentiment of being deprived, this weighs against and sometimes destroys altogether the pleasant impression that the thought of others' pleasure should arouse in us.

The sympathy we feel at the sight of physical pleasures is thus less potent on our souls than that inspired by the sight of pain. But it is important nonetheless to note its existence, as it can be used to explain several phenomena in moral sympathy.

You see, my dear C***, that the first causes of sympathy derive from the sensations caused in us by pleasure and pain, and that it is as sensible beings, first of all, that we are susceptible to feeling sympathy for physical suffering, the most common suffering among men. You will see in the next letter how this sympathy, begun by our sensibility, is completed through reflection. How much we owe sympathy, even in its frailest beginnings! As the first cause of this feeling of humanity, its effects are so precious that it can in part repair the suffering caused by personal interest in large societies; it counters the power of might that we encounter at each step and that centuries of enlightenment can only extinguish through the vices that produced it.[18] In the midst of the shock of so many passions oppressing the weak and fending off the unfortunate, humanity secretly pleads for them from the depths of its heart, and seeks revenge against the injustice of fate by awaking in us the sentiment of natural equality.

18. Whether and how centuries of enlightenment might suffice to achieve this is the theme of Condorcet's *Sketch*.

Chapter 5

Letter II

The sympathy we feel for physical suffering, and which constitutes part of what we call humanity,[1] would be a sentiment too transient to be often useful, my dear C***, were we not capable of reflection, as well as sensation. But because reflection prolongs the ideas brought to us by our senses, it extends and preserves in us the effect of seeing suffering, and it is that, one might say, which makes us truly human. Indeed, reflection will fasten in our souls an instance of suffering that was only present to our eyes for one brief moment, and make us want to be relieved from it and from the unwelcome and painful idea of it. It is reflection which, making up for our natural changeability, forces our compassion into action by presenting it anew with objects that had made only a momentary impression. It is reflection which, when we see someone oppressed by pain, reminds us that we, too, are subject to that same tyrant, destroyer of life, and through emotion and self-pity moves us closer to her, making her sufferings interesting to

---

1. Humanity is an important subject in eighteenth-century moral philosophy distinct from and wider in scope than justice and equity. In Grouchy, humanity seems to start out as a generalized moral pity (and later developed into something wider). For wider reading, see Jacqueline Taylor, "Hume on the Importance of Humanity," *Revue internationale de philosophie* 1 (2013): 81–97; Ryan Patrick Hanley, "David Hume and the "Politics of Humanity," *Political Theory* 39:2 (2011): 205–233; and Marc-Andre Bernier and Deidre Dawson, *Les Lettres sur la Sympathie (1798) de Sophie de Grouchy: philosophie morale et reforme sociale* (Oxford: Voltaire Foundation, 2010), 38n13.

us, even when they are more repulsive than attractive. It is reflection, at last, that by training our sensibility through habit, by extending its activity, makes an active and permanent sentiment out of the humanity in our souls. This sentiment, burning to exercise itself, seeks men's happiness through scientific work, the meditations of nature, experience, or philosophy, or, by attaching itself to suffering and misfortune, follows it everywhere and becomes its comforter, its god. The sentiment of humanity, therefore, is like a seed placed deep in men's hearts by nature, which will germinate and grow through reflection.[2]

But are there not animals, one might ask, that are capable of pity but not reflection?[3]

Let us reply, first, that they are sensitive beings, and that this, as we saw, suffices to render them capable of sympathizing with suffering. Second, we do not know the nature nor the extent of the ideas animals are susceptible to. Consequently we can neither deny nor claim that the degree of compassion they are capable of is the effect of any degree of reflection. And one of the animals upon which the sight of suffering has the greatest power, the dog, is also one of those that seem the least removed from human intelligence.

But if we observe man himself, we will more easily recognize still how he owes the greatest part of his humanity to the faculty of reflection. Indeed, one is human in proportion as one is sensitive and reflective. Those who live in the country, and in general those whose occupations bring them closest to material cares that do not leave time for reflection, are less likely to show compassion than others. One of the principal aims of laws should therefore be to create

---

2. Here, Grouchy seems to depart slightly from Rousseau, who in his *Discourse on the Origins of Inequality*, part I, argues that compassion is prior to reflection and cannot be destroyed by even the most depraved morals. See Jean-Jacques Rousseau, *The Discourses and Other Early Political Writings* (Cambridge: Cambridge University Press, 1997).

3. The question of how closely animals resemble humans was a popular topic, raised by Wollstonecraft, Bentham, and Hume, among others.

and maintain equality of fortune among citizens, bringing to each without exception a degree of ease such that the anxiety caused by the constant awareness of life's necessities and whether they can be met does not render them incapable of such degree of reflection as is necessary for the perfection of all natural sentiments, and particularly that of humanity.

Among the higher class of men who have more freedom and wealth, do we not see also that their degree of humanity depends on the degree of sensitivity, and especially reflection, they are capable of? Are those beings not always devoid of humanity and compassion who are concerned only with the exclusive passions born of egoism or vanity, and which only leave enough attention for their object, and enough reflection for devising the means of obtaining it?

Just as the general impression of suffering on our organs is revived by the sight or the memory of it, it is also reproduced by the abstract idea we have of it and, consequently, by that of the circumstances that follow from it, and of the situations in which it is inevitable. Although that impression is thus ordinarily reproduced in a more vague and indeterminate manner (because the abstract idea of pain brings it less close to us), nonetheless if this idea presents us with a combination of new and extraordinary sufferings, its effect can be equal to that of a present suffering. Such is the cause of the painful sensation we experience when, without thinking about any person in particular, we turn our thoughts to that class of men who, bound at the same time to the hardest labors and to destitution, or at least to the threat of it; or when (without stopping on the idea of a particular suffering or pain) we feel a keen emotion, as we learn that a man has become reduced to destitution by an unanticipated reversal of fortune, or even that he is only threatened by it.

The most abstract idea of a physical pain therefore—that of the possibility of a stranger's suffering—revives with more or less strength the general impression of pain on our organs. The idea of moral suffering produces that same effect. But to account for the sympathy we feel for the moral suffering that is common to all members of our species, we need to go back to the cause of our private sympathies,[4] because these are the causes of our general sympathy.

Let us see first why it is that we tend to sympathize more with the suffering of certain individuals than with the similar or equal pain experienced by others.

Discounting the moral conventions that make up the greatest part of the happiness and existence of those whose minds are developed and exercised, and discounting everything that contributes to a civilized person's happiness, each person finds herself, for all necessities—her well-being and life's comforts—in a particular dependence on many others. This dependence, in truth more widespread and noticeable in childhood, persists to a certain degree with age and retains more or less strength depending on how one's moral development precludes it or allows it to subsist. But because extreme inequality of fortune reduces most men in the social state to provide for their own physical needs, the greatest part of humanity is bound in a state of close dependence on all those who can help satisfy those needs. It follows that each individual soon comes to consider those to whom he owes the greatest part of his existence as the impending and permanent cause of his sufferings or enjoyment, so that their presence and the very idea of them cannot be indifferent to him and will infallibly cause him pain or pleasure.

This particular dependence on a few individuals begins in the crib;[5] it is the first tie binding us to our fellow creatures. It is the reason why an infant's first smiles, and then her more habitual smiles, are

---

4. "[S]ympathies particulières."
5. The idea of the formative importance of infancy was widespread, through popular writings on education by Locke and Rousseau.

for her nurse;[6] it is why she cries when she is not in her nurse's arms, and why for a long time she likes to throw herself upon the breast that satisfied her first needs, made her experience her first sensations of pleasure, and she developed and acquired her first habits.

The strength of our sensibility being dependent on the state we find ourselves in, and the idea of the people to whom we owe the best part of our well-being sufficing in itself to bring about an emotion, we are predisposed to form emotions concerning anything that may happen to them: their pleasures and pains, therefore, must affect us more vividly than the pleasures and pains of others.

Indeed, their suffering must move us more than that of anyone else, because we see those people as tied to us, and because, as they are more often in our sight and in our thoughts, when they suffer, we must be at the same time moved by the idea of their present pain and by that of the consequences of their suffering—the more or less lasting and dreadful pains to which their present state exposes them.

Being accustomed to feel the ties of their existence to ours, we are bound also to feel, at the sight of their suffering or of their enjoyment, a sentiment such as would be caused by the idea of a personal danger or a personal good. And this is solely the result of habit, and does not require any special or reflective attention to our own interest.

Once civilization has achieved a certain level, what we have said about the kind of sympathy we are disposed to feel for people who contribute to our happiness or who help us satisfy our needs extends to two other classes of individuals. The first of these are those we can

---

6. Note that unlike most other writers of that period who were in favor of breastfeeding, (Rousseau, Wollstonecraft), and despite Rousseau's views being highly fashionable especially among aristocratic women, Grouchy does not focus on the natural mother, but simply on whoever happens to be in charge of feeding the infant. On this, see Sandrine Bergès, "Wet-Nursing and Political Participation: The Republican Approaches to Motherhood in Mary Wollstonecraft and Sophie de Grouchy," in *The Social and Political Philosophy of Mary Wollstonecraft*, ed. Sandrine Bergès and Alan Coffee (Oxford: Oxford University Press, 2016), 201–217.

rely on for help and support in the misfortunes that may threaten us.[7] This relationship may seem indistinct, less direct, and physical, perhaps, but it can become tight in certain social conditions, when our fears and hopes are more pressing concerns than our needs, and when we live much in the future. For the second class of individuals, a private sympathy can be established between those who are brought together by their tastes and habits and those who find each other's company fitting and agreeable. And the strength of such sympathy depends on how great a part of happiness is constituted by the fittingness and agreeableness of their company.

We now see how we are disposed to a particular sympathy for those we are tied to by utility or pleasure.[8] We see that the cause of that sympathy, like that which we experience for the physical suffering common to all men, is derived from the general impression of pain and pleasure in our organs, which can itself be awakened by the abstract ideas of pain and pleasure, and can be altered by any circumstance that may influence our sensibility.

Perhaps you have asked yourself, my dear C***, why, in spite of the painful impression diffused by the sight or the idea of pain in our organs, we like to recall the pains we have experienced, those we have witnessed; and not being satisfied with the emotions we obtain from real troubles, we seek new ones in the narratives of the most

7. The idea of stadial development of society is developed in Montesquieu and Smith. It suggests that some parts of her account are relative to some society, while others are general. All are the product of the same underlying laws, but their manifestation will differ according to the stage of development they are at. She supposes that an advanced stage involves interactions with a wider mix of people and also more long-term planning than earlier stages. She articulates the significance of this in the final letters.

8. Although Smith discusses utility (*TMS* IV), the use of "utilité" in Grouchy may also be a reference to Bentham, whose work Grouchy was aware of through her friend Dumond, who worked closely with Bentham as a translator. Another likely source is Cesare Beccaria's 1764 treatise *On Crimes and Punishments*, trans. Graeme R. Newman and Pietro Marongiu, 5th ed. (New Brunswick, NJ: Transaction, 2009), which offered a utilitarian treatment of law and was a very important influence on Bentham.

awful misfortunes and the most heartbreaking situations, born only from imagination. Why do all the affectionate and lively souls, on whom the impression of pain is more unwavering and stronger, like to revive this impression by seeking out those who are unhappy, listening closely to the very details of their misfortune, reading novels and tragedies. Why do they each day seem to need to consume all the power of their sensibility so they may enjoy it?

Here are several reasons for this need.

First, we are clearly moved to concern ourselves with others' troubles so we can relieve them. This desire acts in us without any thought as to whether it is possible to contribute to this relief and before we have had time to see whether it will ever be possible to do so. It is this desire which, when we see a man struggling in the water and about to be swallowed up by it, causes spectators on the shore to reach out with their arms to him with urgency, a sublime movement of nature, which shows in an instant all the power of humanity over our hearts and also all the consequences a legislator could derive from that sentiment, more often weakened than strengthened by our institutions.[9]

Experience has shown us how a distinct knowledge of objects has often been useful, and how important it has been for us not to be mistaken as to their true properties. From this was born in us a sentiment that habit rendered natural and automatic. It is an effect of this sentiment, whose existence we often overlook, that when a confused pattern of ideas comes to our mind, or the vague picture of an event emerges in our imagination, we experience an unpleasant impression which leads us to seek to clarify this pattern or study in depth the event and all its details. This impression is of the same kind as that which we experience at the sight of pain. It stems from

---

9. This throw-away comment is tied to a longer discussion of the place of institutions in civic virtue, found in Letter IV and onward.

the same principle. It is produced by the indistinct idea[10] of an evil which might result from real states of affairs of which we are ignorant. We have in us, therefore, a secret impulse to understand the troubles of others as soon as we suspect their existence, and in general, to study in depth any pattern of ideas, any fact of which we have but an incomplete grasp. And this hidden motive of personal interest—if it is regarding ourselves or, in comparison, regarding others—is not to be dismissed as the cause of man's natural curiosity. As soon as we no longer have to worry about our physical needs, our moral needs start tormenting us and we become susceptible to boredom. A few people (especially those whose souls are open to the tastes, designs, and false pleasures of vanity) only experience boredom, because they crave a more advantageous position than the one they already have, so that the very idea of the possibility of such a position puts them off everything they have and leaves them attracted only to that which they do not have. For the human heart, although hard to please even by those objects from which it derives real enjoyment, is even more greedy and insatiable concerning those objects that can only momentarily elude its needs. Others who do not find new ideas and cannot revive them because the weakness of their minds or their health prevents it, remain in the throes of a discontent derived from the state of their physical constitution, the sufferings they anticipate, and the memory or the idea of their pain.[11] Some even are only tormented by boredom because they have not enough reason or courage to exert their minds, or are not sufficiently experienced or enlightened to realize that the mind is like one of these instruments that overload and tire the hand that carries them without using them. Boredom is thus among the

---

10. The terminology of distinct and indistinct ideas goes back to Descartes; an "indistinct" idea is a vague, imprecise idea.

11. Note that Smith also discusses how good or bad health influences our state of mind (*TMS* IV.1.9, p. 214). But the centrality of boredom in Grouchy's discussion seems to be original.

cruelest of sicknesses that can afflict the human heart; so unbearable is it that in order to avoid it, we do not fear to give ourselves over to painful sensations, and it is the desire to avoid boredom that leads us to seek the proximity of the idea of suffering.

But there is a cause yet more potent, active, and persistent. It is the need we have to be moved, despite the fact that, the causes of suffering being much more numerous than those of pleasure and their intensity greater, we cannot expect as many pleasing sensations as painful ones. This need to be moved does not only belong to those souls whose sensibility and natural activity have acquired the greatest possible development through education, thought, and the experience of passion. It is just as easily found in the masses, though they are almost always insensitive. Is it not, indeed, a sort of attraction to any emotion, even painful, that leads the crowds to gather constantly around scaffolds and to witness there sometimes, in all their horrors, tortures that nearly always bring them to tears?[12] The human heart is, in some ways, drawn to what moves and stirs it: it senses that alien emotions will distract it from the habitual impressions it finds painful or insipid, that will preserve it from boredom. Instead, these emotions will increase the heart's strength, making it more supple, making it easier to receive new impressions, and thereby expanding one of its most fecund sources of enjoyment. Emotion thus seems to suit the soul as exercise does the body, and the respite that follows appears to be the only kind it enjoys.

One must observe, however, that except for a small number of circumstances, these painful emotions we seek are mixed with pleasure and that the impression of the pleasure surpasses, or at least erases, that of the suffering. For instance, when we are about to surrender our souls to great tragic emotions, we know that the allure of the

---

12. In the final *Letters*, Grouchy proposes considerable reforms to criminal punishment, but she does not go so far as Beccaria in advocating abolition of capital punishment.

poetry, the novelty of the situation, the greatness and originality of the characters, the deftness of the direction, the pleasure of enjoying at once the means of the art and the effects it produces—that of enriching our imagination, our memory with images and new ideas, of being moved in a way that is new to us and that sometimes makes us greater, makes us grow in our own eyes—we know at the same time that all this will counterbalance the painful sensations mixed with these pleasures, will erase them, and will outlast them. This is true to such an extent that we rarely seek out this kind of painful emotion unless we are also sustained by the hope of experiencing pleasant ones afterwards. One does not reread novels or see tragedies that end in a sinister catastrophe, unless the beauties of the art and situation, moving us continually from fear to hope, from tears of suffering to tears of joy, make us forget at each instant of these dramatic revolutions the tragic and unhappy outcome of its end.[13]

You see, my dear C***, that if nature has surrounded us with many misfortunes, it has also in a way sought to compensate by making our very sufferings sometimes the source of our deepest enjoyment. Let us praise this sublime relationship we find between the moral needs of a few men and the physical needs of others, between the misfortunes that nature and our vices expose us to and the inclinations of virtue which can only be happy by relieving those vices.

13. As well as a clear familiarity with Dubois and Marivaux, who centrally featured in contemporary discussions of the paradoxical pleasures of fiction, it seems that Grouchy knew Aristotle's *Poetics*, possibly through the Racine "moralized" translation which placed more emphasis on the role of tragedy in creating virtuous citizens.

Chapter 6

Letter III

Our topic today, my dear C***, is personal sympathy[1]—that which creates between men the intimate ties necessary for their perfection and happiness, which brings hearts together and binds them with sweet affection. And because it is grounded in more direct connections than general sympathy, the whole of mankind is susceptible to it, and if cultivated, it may help that multitude of men, who have become impervious to all that does not directly bear on their own existence and happiness, to become sensitive to the sufferings and needs of humanity. For indeed, all parts of our sensitivity are connected to each other, so that when we exercise one, the others also become more refined and more prone to feeling.[2]

This sort of sympathy is set in motion as soon as objects that may excite it are displayed. When we see a man for the first time, we observe his features, we search them for his soul. If his face has any charm or beauty at all, even if it is only distinguished by some

---

1. We translate "sympathie individuelle" in Letter III as "personal sympathy." In Letter IV, Grouchy switches back to "sympathie particulière," which we translate as "private sympathy." This reflects the fact that Letter III talks mostly of friendship and love.

2. Here, Grouchy assumes the existence of a networked mechanism, like the nervous system, that organizes (and is in a certain sense the memory of) an individual's sensitivity. Charles Wolfe (see his "Sensibility as Vital Force or as Property of Matter in Mid-Eighteenth-Century Debates," in *The Discourse of Sensibility*, ed. H. M. Lloyd [Dordrecht: Springer, 2013], 147–170) suggested to us Diderot's view of sensitivity just is this network

singularity or other, we study it carefully, attempting to grasp the impressions that cross it and to tease out those that habitually do so. There is no one whose character we cannot guess at least a little from the first sight of a face enough that we may draw some conclusion, favorable or not, about it.[3] Soon, the impression made by a person's physiognomy is enhanced, altered, or undone by their movements, manners, and words, or by whether their words agree or not with their actions. If in the eyes, which betray the soul, or the voice, which modulates it, or the physiognomy, which tells of their habits and the manners which reveal them, we think we find a character, or the signs of some quality that particularly interest us, whether because they are like ours or because they are among those we most highly approve of, or because together they strike us as extraordinary and engaging, then a feeling of benevolence arises in us toward the person who seems thus gifted.[4] We feel drawn to him, we enjoy thinking about him, and the interest we feel intensifies our observations and increases their accuracy. Sometimes, yet, this first impression is so strong as to confuse us, and it takes over our capacity to observe. In lively souls, the effect of such an impression is to give rise to prejudices that blind those souls, rendering them incapable of right and sometimes even reasonable judgment.

This personal sympathy, which for so long was held to be beyond explanation, is a very natural effect of our moral sensibility. When we see in a man the promise of qualities that please us, we feel drawn to

3. Lavater's work on physiognomy was very popular in revolutionary France. Madame Roland was a fan, although she decried the lack of argument in his book. See Marie-Jeanne Phlipon Roland, *Lettres de Madame Roland (1780–1793)*, 2 vols., ed. Claude Perroud (Paris: Imprimerie Nationale, 1900) 1:334. Grouchy seems content to stay with commonsensical observations, and her own conclusions on the subject are not strong enough to deduce that she put any faith in the scientific theory of Lavater.

4. Here, Grouchy expresses views associated with the now discarded science of physiognomy. For useful background, see Melissa Percival, *The Appearance of Character: Physiognomy and Facial Expression in Eighteenth-Century France*, vol. 47 (London/Leeds: MHRA, 1999).

him. This is because, once alert to the possibility of those qualities, we long for all the rewards we implicitly associate with them. Thus, a necessary effect of the most basic and the least reflective kind of self-love is that we love those whose opinions conform to ours and who thereby raise in our own eyes the value we attach to our own judgments and reassure us that we are not mistaken.[5] Similarly, those who recommend themselves to us by their virtue, their humanity, and their charity interest us either because their memory brings help and support to our plans or projects or because the very idea of the good they have done or might yet do renews in us the emotion usually produced by the sight or anticipation of public happiness or the relief of private unhappiness.

You will perhaps find, my dear C***, that the effect here is too great for its cause, and you will no doubt ask yourself why personal sympathy is sometimes so strong while its motives are so weak and nebulous. Why? Because enthusiasm, mixing with our soul's first observations, extends those observations beyond the point to which our factual knowledge alone is able to bring them. If you observe this moral phenomenon, you will see that it fits intense and sudden personal sympathies, and that it explains them perfectly.

Enthusiasm comes from the degree to which our soul is able to represent to itself, at the same time and in an indeterminate manner, all the pleasures or all the pains we would gain from a particular situation, or from a certain person and our relationship with him or her.[6] This picture brings together in one instant what should in reality span months, years, and sometimes an entire lifetime. Enthusiasm, therefore, conceives of its object in an exaggerated sort of way; and

---

5. This claim plays a role in Grouchy's discussion of pedagogues and rhetoric in Letter IV.
6. See David Hume, "Of Superstition and Enthusiasm" (1742), in *Essays Moral, Political, and Literary*, ed. Eugene F. Miller rev. ed. (Indianapolis, IN: Liberty Fund, 1987). But Grouchy secularizes the concept such that it does not require religiosity.

because it presents the mind with a greater number of objects than it is able to consider distinctly, it is always vague in some respects. Our sensitivity is then subject to another form of amplification born out the multiplication of pains and pleasures we imagine. There is even actual error involved here. We are then often moved by fears and desires that are either impossible in reality or at least cannot be found together; but in the midst of our soul's turmoil, we cannot untangle this impossibility. Habit has a distinct influence on this disposition: if a circumstance or a person has provoked it in us on several occasions, that person or circumstance retains the power of provoking it, independent even of our thinking about it, and we can then consider enthusiasm as a passion of the soul. Fear of dishonor, for instance, is only so powerful because we picture vividly and in one instant all the pain of a life spent in opprobrium.[7] But once thus horrified, the idea of dishonor provokes that same sentiment in us, without reviving all those elements that created it in the first place. In the same way, enthusiasm toward certain qualities disposes us to sudden and rash sympathy for the people in whom we think we recognize them.

This readiness to feel those sudden and intense sympathies thus depends, as enthusiasm does, on:

1. The strength of imagination, which embraces with more or less haste great displays of sensations and events.
2. The strength of sensitivity, which is more or less affected by those displays and preserves them with more or less constancy.

We could add to this any more or less profound reflections we have had about the object of those sympathies. For if by a sort of instinct

---

7. This is a reminder of of the feudal state of late eighteenth-century society, that dishonor played such an important role in Grouchy's moral discussion.

or because of particular circumstances we have given some thought to a situation, an opinion, or a quality, then as we have considered their advantages or disadvantages, our hearts are ready to feel affection toward those people who find themselves in that situation, hold that opinion, or display that quality. The need or desire to find an object for this affection, to exhale a sentiment we have long carried inside our soul without deriving any pleasure from it, produces these sudden sympathies which often seem the result of luck or whim. The nature and the duration of personal sympathies, therefore, depend on the strength of imagination, on sensitivity, and on the measure of thought we have given to their motives.

Such sympathies are born more quickly and seem more intense among those who see and feel with their imagination and whose ideas are in greater turmoil than their sentiments are warmd. That is, they multiply faster among those whose moral sense is more developed. They are more tender according to whether their object is more subtle and pure; for nature dictated, in order to tie us more closely to one another, that the coming together of virtue's affections should be almost as sweet as its deeds.

Sympathies last longer in those whose sensibility has more depth than intensity, more tenderness and delicacy than passion between those who love with that truth, that purity of heart which is as necessary to attraction as to the endurance of these affections. They are more intimate between those melancholy and thoughtful souls who, gratified by their own emotions and enjoying them in silent contemplation, see life only through their affections and remain focused on those without ever desiring more; for as insatiable as the human heart is, true happiness, once recognized, is never exhausted.

It has been said often that respect is the most solid basis for personal sympathy, but the sweetness of that sentiment has not sufficiently been described, the delicacy of the human heart has not been made clear enough. However, respect is necessary for trust and freedom, the first steps toward our soul's well-being. We can only love with the full force of our sensibility within the bounds of respect. It is in a sense the unique environment in which our affections can develop that our hearts grow unconstrained and consequently whole. For honest souls, respect is always implicit in personal sympathies, and can even be their sole cause where its objects are a few extraordinary qualities, because then real pleasure can be derived from it.

The honorable man loves to honor; his heart, easily moved by the very idea of a good deed, finds itself bound to those he believes capable of such deeds. He enjoys their company, and this fraternity of virtue establishes between them liberty and equality—as sweet a feeling, perhaps, as the closer ties of blood and nature.[8]

The first movements of sympathy for someone we hardly yet know, brought about by physiognomy, manners, or snippets of conversation, are enough to bring us pleasure. Respect alone is sufficient to bring about a feeling of goodwill and freedom, that first sentiment of happiness which disposes us to experience others. But sympathy, we see, is made sweeter by better foundations and stronger feelings, and this explains the attraction of friendship. The attraction begins before even friendship is established, and as soon perhaps as we begin to think it possible. As soon, indeed, as we conceive of the possibility of a person who might love us, with deep and delicate affections, we experience a delicious feeling, collecting in our soul thoughts of all the pleasures that friendship can produce. This feeling itself is pleasurable, and this is why, even though we respond to physical pain and pleasure, the pleasure of loving and being loved is itself a form of happiness.

The pleasure that comes from loving is also partly born of the enjoyment we derive from the idea, the memory, or the hope of procuring happiness through our affection to a sensitive being. If this

8. Note Grouchy's reinterpretation of the motto of the French Revolution.

person is often near us, if our enthusiasm intensifies the happiness he derives from our friendship, as well as the happiness we may derive from it, then the pleasure we have in loving him grows. And when we have felt this pleasure often enough that our sensibility feels its attraction and comes to need it, the person who is the source of that friendship becomes dearer to us, and what we feel for him becomes a necessary part of our existence.

So much is it the case (at least as far as friendship is concerned) that the greatest cause of the pleasure we derive from loving is in making others happy through our affection, a love which only generous souls are capable of giving. People who are neither inspired nor honorable, or who are corrupted by egoism, can desire to be loved and seek the pleasures and benefits it would bring them, but it is only generous hearts, capable of being moved by others' happiness, who know how to love. The meeting of opinions, taste, character, and all the other motives of personal sympathy may bring men closer and unite their hearts in appearance, but it is only the faculty of enjoying others' happiness that brings about solid, true, and lasting affections, independent of place, time, interest, and ability to render life pleasant and delightful.[9] When with care we exercise and cultivate in children's souls their natural sensitivity to other people's pleasures, and especially the happiness they derive from contributing to it, we do not just dispose them to acquire the most pleasant or useful virtues; we also ensure that they will be capable of loving, that they will feel all the delights of love, or at least be worthy of them.

Beauty (whatever the true origins of beauty might be; here it is only taken to mean that which we enjoy looking at) inspires by its sight alone a pleasurable feeling. A beautiful person holds, in the eyes of all, the power to contribute to the happiness of all who surrounds him or her. We tend to give beautiful people's words,

9. Grouchy's defense of love owes much to Hobbes and Mandeville.

manners, feelings, and deeds more weight simply because they are more delightful people: we love them naturally. This feeling, together with those born out of physiognomy and the qualities of the soul, gives rise to a particular feeling we call *romantic love*.[10] This especially differs from other feelings, in that it produces a pleasurable sensation that the sight or thought of that person who inspired it always renews. This power of granting us happiness at each instant, of drawing, engaging, binding, filling our senses completely, if only by arousing them, has a greater hold on the whole of mankind than either the pleasures of friendship or the charms found in the company of virtuous men.[11] We cannot doubt but that beauty, or at least some pleasant and interesting features, are necessary for love. Exceptions to this are rare among men, and their taste for pleasure is almost always the reason for it. If the exceptions are somewhat less rare among women, this is because of moral notions of modesty and duty, which from childhood lead women to be watchful of their first impressions, so that they are not determined by good looks alone but, rather, nearly always show a preference for moral qualities and sometimes even propriety. Romantic love may come about through a diversity of causes, and it is greater as it has more of them. Sometimes our senses are moved and even overcome by a single attraction or quality; often (too often), they are lured by attributes that have nothing to do with the heart. But when they are more subtle and enlightened, they fix on the combination of all that can satisfy them, and with a tact equal to that of reason and prudence, they give in to love only if it is the very best of what love has to offer. Then love becomes a real passion, even in the purest souls, even in those who are the least slave to their

---

10. I translate *amour* as "romantic love." *Amour* is italicized in the original.

11. Bernier and Dawson (*Lettres sur la Sympathie*, 53n29) note that Grouchy takes romantic love more seriously than does Smith. According to them, Smith thinks love is ridiculous because it is impossible to understand, and he believes that friendship depends only on virtue.

impressions and sensual needs. Then innocent caresses can suffice for a long time and lose nothing of their charm after they are over; then the happiness of being loved is the most necessary of pleasures, the most desired; then all thoughts of love and sensual delight are born of a single object, depending on it always and obliterates all others.[12]

But love can only be all that when two souls know each other perfectly, so that their union is unreserved, their love is boundless in its trust, and they hold in respect all that they care for. To love an individual is to love his entire existence, its imperfections as well as its qualities and charms. In our failures as in our successes, at times when we need consoling for the trials and the knowledge of men, at those when we find it hard simply to enjoy life, he who has charmed our existence must become a restorative, a guide to our happiness. In particular, the happy connection of character, mind, and heart between two individuals must preserve the happiness of this union from the natural fickleness and the bold aspirations of the human heart.

The reciprocity of personal sympathy depends on which of a variety of causes it is born of; it cannot fail when sympathy is based on conformity of taste, opinion, and especially emotional response. But even independent of such conformity, sympathy can often be reciprocal; it is then derived from the attraction that naturally draws us to those who love us. And the fact that it has different origins in the two people it brings together does not lessen its strength. To love is therefore a reason for being loved, unless extraordinary circumstances had previously captured our senses exclusively, so that sympathy cannot be reciprocal. But in the ordinary sense, the term "sympathy" includes the idea of reciprocity.[13]

---

12. This is, in fact, also Smith's position; *TMS* III.1.7, p. 113, and III.5.8, p.166; Smith adds that we also want to feel that we deserve to be *beloved*.

13. The reciprocal nature or mutuality of sympathy has a long history; see Eric Schliesser, "Introduction: on Sympathy," in *Sympathy: A History* (Oxford: Oxford University Press, 2015), 9ff.

Such reciprocity is rarer where passionate love is concerned, because even the purest of loves is the result of attraction that is in large part independent of the moral qualities that give rise to sympathy in other forms of attachment. A sweet physiognomy delights, stirs, and inspires love, but what distinguishes such love from friendship is precisely how the sight or the memory of this physiognomy always renews in us this pleasure. If love itself is to be reciprocal, therefore, some of the causes of its attraction must be, too—at least in some respects. Perhaps the sources of such reciprocity are common enough in nature, but they are scattered, and one senses how rarely they must meet or at least how unlikely it is that these causes should be absolutely alike, or of equal strength in the two people they bring together.

Let us now inquire as to what degree of sympathy is necessary to feel toward the people we meet often in order to find their company pleasant and desirable.

It seems to me, my dear C***, that sympathy born out of respect is not sufficient for this, for by *respect*, we usually mean only that cool interest we have for everyday kindness, austere virtues, or a few dazzling intellectual traits.[14] But this sort of interest has only a weak power of attraction (unless it is carried to the highest degree, which is rare). But also, any quality or perfection must be accompanied by understanding, gentleness, and kindness so as not to obstruct our independence or make us too conscious of our own weakness. What the human heart needs first of all is freedom; if it is to be just and happy at the same time, it must develop emotional ties to what it respects.[15]

---

14. It seems as though Grouchy is marking her distance with Aristotelian theories of friendship, which were so important, for instance, in Wollstonecraft's theory of love (and earlier in the writings of Lucrezia Marinella; see Marguerite Deslauriers, "Marinella and Her Interlocutors, Hot Blood, Hot Words, Hot Deeds," *Philosophical Studies* 174:10 [2017]: 2525–2537).

15. The emphasis on freedom here serves as reminder that Grouchy was a revolutionary republican. See also the end of Letter VII, where she discusses the place of freedom in marriage and divorce.

It is unfortunate, no doubt, that the virtues most admirable are often those we can least expect indulgence from. The man of sensibility, therefore, can only love those qualities of the mind that are accompanied by virtues; he can only love those virtues that are sentiments rather than opinions, made lovable and moving through indulgence, that seek only to be imitated through being felt, and that we cannot see in others without feeling their power, even though we may have never acted on them.[16]

The kind of sympathy necessary for friendship does not always require the pleasing qualities, the gentle virtues without which a less intimate relationship has no charm. Often, as we are attracted by the particular knowledge of a very rare merit or by a person capable of moving our sensibility, as we become attached, little by little we forget any imperfections attending it. It is often for this reason that people with very different tastes and characters come together. This idiosyncrasy often occurs between souls who, more private and less confiding, exhibit their charm and sensitivity only when entranced by another person. These souls give themselves over exclusively to their affections, which makes these affections sweeter still and even more greatly prized, and they do not require further attraction in order to reciprocate. Although these souls are more susceptible to constancy and passion, their sentiments require a deep and intimate sympathy if they are to last. Love, carried to that degree of strength when it is properly called passion, is a succession of desires, needs, and expectations that must constantly be satisfied, and that bring pleasure even as they fill the soul with turmoil, because this very turmoil becomes a habitual emotional state, always mixed with a degree of happiness. The meeting of minds, as well as of hearts, of taste and opinion, the sweetness of feeling everything together and everything for each other, is the only means of satisfying the workings of love at

16. See *TMS* III.2.17, p. 122.

the heart of happiness and of keeping its charms alive—as love might otherwise die. The pleasures of the mind, the arts, virtue, when taken in the midst of the pleasures of the heart, make these charms deeper and more intense. In the current state of our civilization, they are a necessity, even, for these pleasures to last, and they add to these pleasures a thousand diverse charms. They purify them, enrich and renew them; they make them last throughout the ages of life.

So far, my dear C***, I have shown how moral pains and pleasures are born out of physical sympathy that has become personal, strengthened by diverse circumstances, rendered more active and energetic by enthusiasm. But the origins of this sympathy for another person do not depend on the nature of that person's pains or pleasures. We suffer when we see that person suffer, and the thought of his torments makes us suffer because we feel that the same torment would hurt us, too. It is clear, therefore, that what we have found to be true of physical pains will also be true of moral pains, provided we are subject to them. The sight, the memory of the moral suffering of another affects us like the sight or the memory of his physical suffering.

Here are, therefore, new ties of sympathy by which we are united to mankind, as well as to a wider range of human relationships.

Not only is the sight or memory of others' pains and pleasures, moral or physical, matched in us by pain and pleasure of our own, but as I have already explained, this sensibility, once awakened, can be renewed in us simply by the abstract idea of good and evil.[17] This results in a personal motivation to do good and to avoid doing evil, a motivation that follows from the fact we are *sensitive beings capable of reasoning*, and that can, in subtle souls, serve at once as a guide to the conscience and a prime mover of virtue.

17. This is a key innovation from Grouchy that goes beyond Smith's arguments.

Chapter 7

Letter IV

You see now, my dear C***, that we feel sympathy for physical pains and pleasures in proportion to our understanding of their strengths and consequences,[1] such as we have gained by experiencing them ourselves; in the same way, we are in general more sympathetic toward those moral pains and pleasures we are likely to experience.[2] I say in general, as no doubt some souls are sensitive enough that they may be moved by pains they could not be subject to, even in circumstances that would cause others to experience them—that is, pains that can only be grasped through the imagination. And then, just as it is for physical pains we have not experienced, our sympathy is roused by the idea of unspecified suffering.

This opinion contradicts that of the famous Smith, and I will argue with him on a few more points yet. You will perhaps find me rather daring, but even if Smith is rightly considered one of the foremost philosophers in Europe, when the topic is self-knowledge rather than one that requires extensive learning, it seems to me that all who are capable of thought are entitled to join the debate.[3]

---

1. Thus, sympathy is not always merely an automatic fellow feeling; it can also require an evaluation of the intensity and aptness of another's feelings.
2. Here, Grouchy is in agreement with Aristotle (*On Rhetoric*, trans. George A. Kennedy [Oxford: Oxford University Press, 2006], 1387a); and *TMS* III.3.4, p. 157.
3. This is a nice expression of standpoint epistemology.

I do not believe that Smith has given the true reason why we pity dethroned kings.[4] If we have more compassion for their misfortunes than for those of others, it is only because kings who seem to have been preserved from misfortune by their elevation strike us as more sensitive to them. It is not (as Smith believes) because the idea of greatness, joined in the thoughts of many to the idea of happiness, disposes us, through a sort of affection and indulgence toward their well-being, to sympathize with them more closely. It seems to me that this affection is not widely spread in the British Empire, that it is absent from the rest of Europe, and that in any case it is clearly opposed to the sentiment of natural equality that causes us to feel envy,[5] or at least a certain harshness, toward everything that is above us.

Our sympathy for physical suffering is stronger, more general, and more painful than our sympathy for moral suffering. Witnessing such pains can even be undesirable and distressing for those whose education—or, rather, the errors of their education—protected them from seeing others suffer. This is obviously due to the very nature of physical suffering, the fact that it more often leads to death, that it is more extraordinary, its symptoms more explicit, so that the sight of it is more painful and more likely to cause our organs to respond in sympathy.

Smith asserts a contrary proposition and thinks he can justify it by claiming that the imitation of bodily suffering does not move— that it is an object of ridicule, not compassion, whereas the imitation of moral suffering rouses more vivid impressions in one's soul. Is it because we feel less sympathy for a man whose leg is amputated than for a man who loses his mistress that the latter but not the former is a proper object for tragedy? Certainly not: it is only because it would

4. *TMS* I.3.2, p. 63.
5. It is "jalousie" in the text.

be too difficult to create the illusion necessary to stage a successful imitation of such physical pain; because, for the sake of variety and keeping us interested, this imitation needs to be accompanied by moral suffering.[6] Finally, it is because the point of tragedy is in great part to make our sympathy for the misfortunes of others seem pleasant to us by stimulating our sensibility progressively, and not by suddenly confronting it with the heartbreaking sight of physical pain—a sight we cannot stop thinking about if it moves us, and which turns into ridicule if it doesn't. In any case, we know that the spectacle of physical suffering is a real tragedy for the masses, a tragedy they seek only through a dumb curiosity, but whose sight sometimes arouses the kind of sympathy that can become a passion to contend with.[7]

It is absolutely false that strength and courage in the experience of bodily pain arise from the fact that such pain inspires little sympathy in others (as Smith claims it does). Resignation in ordinary suffering comes from the necessity and sometimes even the usefulness of the pain itself and from the futility of complaining. But for pain that consumes our whole strength, fortitude arises from the desire to be admired or the feeling of contentment that comes from courage— which often perpetuates it and can become an intense pleasure for strong and high-minded souls.

Smith claims that we have very little sympathy for the pleasures of love. If he means by this that we do not care for the delights granted young lovers by a pure and deep sentiment, or the secret sanctuary that such a sentiment draws them to, that we do not care to hear about the details of a happiness we secretly wish for, then his opinion will be in contradiction to that of all those who have a sensitive

6. This observation lends itself to an interesting discussion of the rules of tragedy (no death on stage) and the use of special effects in horror cinema.
7. Less than a year after she wrote these words, Sophie would travel with the crowds going to the guillotine, in order to visit her husband in hiding.

imagination and who have once experienced such passion. A happy love story—real or imagined—that excites neither envy nor jealousy, that does not offend modesty nor our principles of honesty, will gratify us and arouse in us pleasurable sensations.[8] It will please us even when it saddens us, as those who have once felt or inspired such passion long afterward find pleasure in those tender and sometimes painful regrets. Because sympathy for others' happiness comes before envy and before concerns for honesty and modesty, if any such concern or envious reaction prevents us from sympathizing with the joys of love, we should not conclude that such sympathy is not natural. We should observe only that our sympathy with these pleasures is proportionate to the severity of our principles, their complexity, and our propensity to share easily in pleasures that we have never experienced or of which we are currently deprived.

It comes as a surprise that love's passion should always appear somewhat ridiculous to a philosopher[9] who has shown throughout his work that he has observed man in nature and society without prejudice. One would rather impute such an opinion to frivolous youths with their propensity to judge love before they have loved, and who are convinced that they are on the path to true happiness because they will not accept any trouble in exchange for their pleasure.

As a general rule, we do not feel sympathy for passions such as hatred, envy, revenge, and so on. Rather, it depends on the personal ties we have with the person who is prey to these passions; on the particular sympathy we have for that person, which may corrupt our judgment; on the justice of their sentiments, which may appeal to us with more or less strength and recognition; on whether the cause that moves them touches our own interests, our opinions, and the

8. By contrast, Smith had claimed that is "the misfortunes of lovers . . . which interest us upon the theatre" (*TMS* I.3.2.2, p. 52).
9. See *TMS* I.2.2.1, p. 31.

nature of our sensitivity. When any of these particular motivations fail to excite our sympathy, it becomes instead a milder sentiment—pity. And rather than sympathize with those hateful passions, we become concerned, instead, for the person they are directed toward. This tendency is fortunately derived from nature: we feel sympathy for those who desire to help others because we, too, have this desire to benefit all, so that perceiving it in others gives us a certain personal enjoyment. And we do not feel sympathy for hatred because, as we do not have in us a general desire to hurt everyone, we would need a particular reason to feel sympathy for the hatred, as indeed we would for hating. If this is true, you may ask, my dear C***, why there are people who enjoy seeing others being hurt, who somehow need to seek revenge from others' happiness, and who experience a secret joy whenever they hear of someone else's sorrow? Why? Because in society a vicious system of legislation, instead of bringing together the interests of individuals, has for a long time now only separated them and set them against each other. Their greed for pleasure has led men to the point where it is impossible for all to satisfy these social fantasies that, now turned into habits, have usurped the title of needs. As children, they tacitly become habituated to count the fortunes and misfortunes of others as a personal gift to themselves or something taken from them to give others.[10] Civilized man, therefore, when he is ruled by prejudices and bad laws, is naturally envious and jealous, and more so depending on how far the vices of social institutions pull him from nature, corrupt his reason, and make his happiness dependent on the satisfaction of a greater number of needs.[11]

10. Contrast with Letter I, where Grouchy discusses her own education.
11. This whole paragraph can be read as a commentary on Rousseau's *Discourse on Inequality*. Although society under bad laws is corrupting, good laws and knowledge would produce a harmony of interests and mutual love in society for civilized man.

There is so much truth in this that even those who are guilty of finding pleasure in others' misfortunes and pain in their happiness only do so in relation to accidents of vanity or fortune, or those they believe to be faked or exaggerated. But in the absence of personal hatred or in the presence of physical pain and real misfortune, these feelings disappear. Exceptions to this observation are extremely rare and only befall a very small number of individuals: monsters whose existence may be accounted for by the particular circumstances of their education and social situation.[12] Civilization, such as it still exists in half of all European nations, is therefore the enemy of human goodness and happiness. So much work is to be done by educators, not to develop or control nature but to preserve its benevolent tendencies, to prevent their being smothered by those prejudices so commonly accepted, which corrupt at their very source our sentiments of humanity and equality—sentiments that are as necessary to the moral happiness of each individual as they are to the preservation of justice and security in all aspects of the social order!

Our tendency to imitate those who laugh at the faults of others and ridicule them is probably born of sympathy. But what is the cause of the amusement brought about by the sight of ridicule? Does the sight of ridicule inspire in us the pleasure our pride derives from an idea of our own superiority? Indeed, pleasurable pride is sometimes one of the causes of such amusement, but it is not the main one. As we often observe, satisfied pride usually manifests itself in a discreet smile. It seems we would fear to lose the sense of dignity that is typical of this sentiment if we abandoned ourselves to the brash displays of laughter caused by the sight of ridicule. Indeed, the sense of our

12. This may be a reference to the Marquis de Sade. Smith treats Monsters, as "what is perfectly deformed, are always most singular and odd, and have the least resemblance to the generality of that species to which they belong" (*TMS* V.1.8, p. 232). For Grouchy, a monster can look like the rest of us but be deformed by status or education.

own superiority brings us a very different sort of pleasure from that produced by the sight of ridicule; and this pleasure makes us seem ridiculous more often than when it is born of others' ridicule.

The organic movements of laughter are by their nature pleasant, although they are sometimes tiring, and when they cause tears, they are tiresome; but under certain conditions, tears may bring relief. This observation shows in part why we feel sympathy for laughter caused by ridicule, but not why the objects of ridicule set laughter and the pleasure that precedes it into motion.

Children laugh very early; they learn to laugh as soon as they have sufficiently distinct and widespread knowledge of objects to be able to compare them. They laugh at the same things we do, since in their games they laugh at those they manage to trick. It must be, therefore, that the cause of this phenomenon is not too complicated nor requires too much knowledge; indeed, even the simple-minded can laugh, and they laugh at what surprises them in the same way that sensible people laugh at what they find pleasant.

Because children have fewer ideas, and more limited ideas, we must therefore look for the causes of laughter in them, as we will have fewer causes to examine and more hope of finding the correct ones. This method of searching for the origins of facts (which we owe to Locke)[13] is the best way of finding the general law those facts are subject to.

It appears that the most common cause of laughter in children is that they are struck by an unexpected event that gives them new images and ideas, and that exercises their growing faculties in a vigorous manner. Every time in such circumstances that they feel pleasure or hope, laughter follows because it is the natural expression of every

---

13. See "Historical, Plain Method," in Locke, *Essay Concerning Human Understanding*, 1.1.2. This is, in fact, an innovation over Locke. For Locke, hidden (real) essences expressed themselves in manifest ways. For Grouchy, facts fall under general laws.

pleasure they experience. But as we grow older and more thoughtful, we only laugh at the unexpected, at those things that entertain without inspiring great interest. The reason for this is simple: the convulsions of laughter and the pleasure that accompanies them give way to the slightest exertion of the mind, and the unexpected things that please us without being followed by reflection of any sort are extremely rare after childhood. It is for this reason that laughter is, later in life (except for the simple-minded), reserved nearly exclusively for the bizarre, the unexpected, the incongruous—and ridicule belongs to this category.

The first cause of laughter, therefore, comes from the easy and unexpected exercise of our faculties, in the sort of satisfaction or interior joy that accompanies it, and it is uncomplicated. Later on in life, laughter and mockery often go together because, as we gather pleasure from our advantages and our strengths, we are led to feel a malicious pleasure in making our superiority felt. This is a pleasure similar to the one resulting from the exercise of our faculties.

You will forgive, my dear C***, my moving from cause to cause until I find the first cause, and having observed as I have that the cause of laughter generally owes much to the pleasure attached to the exercise of our faculties, you will perhaps be as keen as I am to seek the origins of that pleasure.

It may suffice, in order to discover it, to note that the exercise of our faculties helps perfect them, and that by perfecting them, we gain pleasure and avoid pain. Even children observe this, better than we do, because their faculties are rapidly improved and their well-being depends greatly upon it. A pleasurable feeling, therefore, automatically follows any exercise of our faculties that helps develop them.

This pleasurable sentiment, which is the same as the one we derive from in feeling our own strength (by which I mean *power* or *capacity*), may seem weak at first sight because, often, habit robs us of it. However, it is very vigorous, as children demonstrate. The sole exercise of their faculties, independent of any pleasure they may find in it, brings out in them all the symptoms of happiness. The more they cultivate it, the easier they will find happiness in later life. What matters most at first is to limit their existence to that sentiment for as long as possible. What is most essential next is not to let them acquire an exaggerated opinion of their own strength. If they acquire an opinion of it that, when they compare themselves to others it is not exactly right, and does not fall within its true worth, that this childhood self-love, blindly cherished by us, will become in them the source of all the mind's defects and the heart's vices.

But there are other causes yet for the pleasure we derive from exercising our faculties. The exercise of our bodily faculties is not only good for our health but it also nearly always produces a sense of well-being, a sensation that always accompanies a state of healthy existence and that, if not a positive pleasure, is at least the recent and pleasant cessation of all painful feeling. Not only does this feeling affect the body as a whole, but after some reflection we can see that it resonates separately in each organ. We find pleasure in walking after a long period of rest; upon noticing this pleasure, we find that the sensation felt in the body as a whole is also felt more particularly in the legs.

This observation applies not only to our bodily faculties but also to the organs affected by thought and sentiment.

If concentrating too hard is tiring, it is likely that a long period without receiving new ideas is even more unpleasantly tiring. And if experiencing lively emotions, even joy, causes us to feel pain in the *diaphragm*,[14] is it not also likely that the total absence of any sentiment should lead to a painful numbness?

It seems, therefore, that movement and action contribute essentially to the well-being and even the preservation of living beings. This

14. Emphasis in the original.

is conclusively demonstrated by the fact that in childhood, movement and action are necessary for the development of our organs, and in old age, to the conservation of their strength.

Because movement and action are necessary for our well-being and preservation, it follows that the exercise of our faculties must be pleasurable, and that it must be so even before reflection teaches us that exercising these faculties will lead to further pleasures. And the improvement that is needed for us to become capable of this degree of reflection is motivated in a way by the pleasure that comes with action, movement, and the exercise of our faculties.

Let us come back to sympathy.

I cannot agree with Smith that we do not sympathize with either great joys or petty sorrows.[15] It seems to me, on the contrary, that we sympathize with moral pains and pleasures, whatever their strength and degree. This follows from what we have so far observed regarding our moral sensitivity. Our sympathy for great joys and petty sorrows may be very deep when it concerns people we have a strong particular sympathy for. There, we obey nature. On the contrary, we are sometimes distressed to witness a man to whom we are indifferent make a great fortune, either because this fortune destroys the equality that existed between us or eliminates the superiority we had over him—or, because we had hoped to benefit from that fortune ourselves. But if a person inferior to us moves up a social class while remaining still far below us, then sympathy, not pride will win. This shows that sympathy exists even when it is stifled by personal interest. This is true to such an extent that even when personal interest has defeated sympathy—and it can only be faked—it still strikes us as a proper and natural sentiment.[16]

---

15. "We are generally disposed to sympathize with small joys and great sorrows" (*TMS* I.2.4.3, p. 50).

16. Smith also thinks this, but the example he gives is of our sympathy for the rich and famous (and he treats it as a corruption of moral sentiments); see *TMS* I.3.2.2, pp. 52–53..

Our sympathy for moral misfortunes is stronger than for moral pleasures, for the same reason that our sympathy for physical pain is stronger than it is for physical pleasure. However, we can observe that even though these sorts of pain are much more intense than corresponding pleasures, the difference is slighter than in the case of physical pain and pleasure. We also observe that moral pleasures have a much greater influence on our happiness than physical ones.

Among the effects of sympathy, we can count the power that a large crowd has to affect our emotions and the power a few men have to inspire opinions. Here are, I believe, a few causes of these phenomena.[17]

First, the very presence of a crowd acts upon us through the impressions created by their faces, discourses, or the memory of their deeds. The attention of the crowd commands our attention, and its eagerness, forewarning our sensibility of the emotions it is about to experience, sets those in motion.[18]

It is also perhaps the pleasure of hearing someone express what we did not dare express, what we perhaps sought in vain, or what we only half-perceived.

It is, again, the pleasure of acquiring here and now an idea or sentiment, a pleasure that when very intense leads us, if we accept such an idea or sentiment without thinking it through, to develop a sudden admiration for the person who inspired it. Doesn't he who gives you a new idea appear to you, my dear C***, vested with supernatural powers?

The last two causes I mentioned will also be effective for the solitary reader, but less so.

---

17. The structure of this letter is odd. Grouchy is mixing topics that she treats separately elsewhere, including crowd psychology, the problem of tragedy, and moral cultivation. It's also a great deal longer than the other letters.

18. This seems borrowed Seneca's 7th Letter to Lucilius, in *Epistles*, vol. 1, trans. Richard Gunmere, Loeb Classical Library (Cambridge, MA: Harvard University Press, 1917).

Having uncertain ideas or sentiments sometimes creates a need to see them shared by others before we give ourselves over to them. An idea may strike us as true, beautiful, and moving; but we worry that we are adopting it too quickly; to hear it applauded reassures us, makes up our minds, and then we confidently give ourselves over to our first impression. Other times, this same applause brings us some idea that had previously eluded us. Our own ideas in turn have the same effect, and each of us is then able to enjoy the shared pleasures.

One man, by himself, fearing ridicule or danger, or just out of timidity, may not dare let himself be gripped by a violent emotion, but he does dare to do so as soon as the emotion is shared.

Finally, as we sympathize with others' passions, the external signs of these passions move us and can by themselves cause us to experience them. So, when we are already moved by them, witnessing them in others makes them grow stronger. And as we too affect others, it must be the case that those passions will keep on growing until they reach the highest degree according to the nature of each. This is what makes the crimes and virtues of popular movements so powerful.

The power some people hold over those who hear or read their words, through a manipulation of the dispositions of their soul, is also an effect of sympathy. It is the result of an art more dangerous than it is difficult, but only until it is exposed.

These people know that some minds are weary of doubt, that they are at rest only when they believe—for some, this is true of a few objects and for others, for all of them. And they know that the need to believe is stronger in most people than reason, which tells us to believe only that which is proven.[19] All that needs to be done, then, is to offer an opinion forcefully and persuasively, artfully hiding what

19. Grouchy lost her faith in her late teens, while reading Voltaire and Rousseau at her convent finishing school (somewhat paradoxically).

may render it dubious. Happily delivered from doubt, most people will embrace this opinion ardently and will find it most striking in proportion to the peace of mind it brings them.

One can also inspire belief and trust in one's person and in ways of thinking by adopting opinions that are welcomed more greedily because they answer a secret desire to give oneself over to them. This is the cause of the success achieved by those who write about paradoxes. That we are vain about having an opinion that is out of the ordinary, about seeing—even through someone else's eyes—what others did not see, is a secret charm that such writers nurture in their readers' minds. We succeed in the same manner by rejuvenating old opinions; this wins us the support of all those who felt forced to abandon those old opinions and did not dare to defend them. These people find pleasure in minimizing the achievements of those who seek to destroy prejudices and put forward new truths, as such projects are always qualified as foolhardy by mediocre people who, for the sake of their self-esteem, seek to render those new truths suspect, and who can never forgive them because such projects show a superiority they find humiliating.

Another means of winning over minds (perhaps the most effective of all) is to take well-known principles, and especially opinions widely and enthusiastically accepted, and add to them opinions that by no means follow from them: the latter commands respect for the former. Also, we tend to believe a writer who agrees with us about important topics and who defends opinions we care about. This is so much the case that sometimes it is enough to use a few key words to inspire a sort of worship and enthusiasm through the grand thoughts the words suggest. The art of putting together words in such a way as to replace reason and thinking, to produce in the minds of readers or spectators such an effect as to make them incapable of reasoning, is one of the best-kept secrets of false eloquence, and it is responsible for the short-lived fame of more than one of our political orators.

The success of true talent, which is entirely the work of nature, is even simpler to account for. If a writer or an orator expresses himself passionately, then we necessarily experience that emotion caused by seeing a person moved by an intense and deep emotion. And this feeling, which automatically answers to that writer's or orator's, disposes us to share it, providing we feel that it has sufficient cause. The power such men have over us is not limited to making us feel strongly what we would only otherwise feel meekly but also works on our opinions. If we analyze carefully the causes of our beliefs, we will see that one of the strongest and most usual is the natural propensity to believe that repetition entails constancy. And this propensity is derived from our constitution. We think of what we have experienced consistently as general and permanent; when we do not think, we sometimes confuse the impression we get from something habitually repeated with the impression we get from something striking us vividly. And out of this confusion arises a great ease for believing whatever moves us— and for adopting the opinions of passionate writers.

Such is the art of Rousseau, their model.[20] He penetrates you with his own conviction and, in a moment, excites in the depths of your heart an emotion with much pull toward the opinion he wants to establish—as would be the habitual impression of all that is capable of justifying this opinion. One of his contemporaries, perhaps, has had an even more striking and general influence on the century, outside of France at least. But if the methods of both were equally crowned with success, they yet were not the same. Rousseau spoke to our conscience; Voltaire, to reason. Rousseau established his opinions through the force of his sensibility and of his logic; Voltaire, through his lively charm and wit. One instructed men by moving them, and the other by enlightening and amusing them at the same

---

20. Note that the point of view changes several times in this paragraph and the previous one; "their" refers to the orators, whose style of writing is modeled on Rousseau's.

time. The first, having taken certain of his principles too far, has given us a taste for exaggeration and peculiarity; the second, too often satisfied with using ridicule as a weapon against the worst abuses, has not succeeded in rousing that healthy indignation that, while less efficacious than scorn in punishing vice, is nonetheless more active in fighting it. Rousseau's morality is engaging, if severe, and it moves the heart even while it disciplines it. Voltaire's more indulgent morality is perhaps less moving, and because it requires fewer sacrifices, it gives us a lower opinion of our own strength and of the perfection we are capable of reaching. Rousseau talked of virtue with as much charm as Fénelon and derived his influence from virtue itself.[21] Voltaire fought religious prejudice with as much zeal as if it had been the sole enemy of our happiness. The first will renew, age after age, our enthusiasm for liberty and virtue; the second will alert each century to the deadly effects of fanaticism and credulity. However, as passions will live as long as mankind, Rousseau's influence on our souls will still affect our ways, long after Voltaire's influence on our minds will have destroyed the prejudices that prevent the happiness of societies.

21. François de Salignac Fénelon, *The Adventures of Telemachus*, ed. Patrick Riley (Cambridge: Cambridge University Press, 1994). This was a work that greatly influenced the political writings of the eighteenth century in France. It is arguable, in particular, that much of Rousseau's rural republicanism came from Fénelon.

Chapter 8

Letter V

On the Origins of Moral Ideas

It seems to me, my dear C***, that the preachers of virtue (Rousseau excepted) rarely seek to unearth the origins of moral ideas. Yet it is through this inquiry alone that we may come to understand the intimate ties that exist between those ideas and our conscience and between the feelings we experience when we act according to them and our happiness.[1] It follows that although the immediate influence of vice and virtue on our well-being has been praised often and eloquently, it has not sufficiently been argued that the principles of virtue and the personal happiness they procure are a necessary consequence of our moral constitution, and that the need to be virtuous is practically irresistible for those who are ruled by wise laws and raised without prejudices.

Because witnessing the pleasure of others, or even the idea of someone else's pleasure naturally satisfies us, it necessarily follows that we experience pleasure when we are the cause of it in another. It is stronger than the sort of pleasure we cause in others because it is more thoughtful and deliberate, and because it is anticipated, which

---

1. "Moral" is contrasted with "physical;" "moral ideas" are ideas about society. But as Grouchy notes, there is an intimate connection between such ideas and morality.

always increases the mind's activity. If we get more pleasure from contributing to others' happiness than we do from witnessing it, then that pleasure must be greater still when we relieve someone of their trouble. Such pleasure is enjoyed more thoughtfully and is always accompanied by the pleasant sensation of being delivered from the idea of pain. The enjoyment of performing a good deed is increased by this also: knowing that we owe the pleasure that follows from it to our own agency, that we have, consequently, the power to secure it for ourselves and to replicate it at will. For although possession may sometimes make something that was once pleasing no longer attractive to us, it is more striking still that in a simple and natural life, possession increases something's value—for it brings together the present and the future, the current pleasures and those derived from reliable expectations.

Performing good deeds, therefore, naturally brings us pleasure. But another sentiment is born out of that pleasure: the satisfaction of having done good. This is similar to the way physical pain, as well as a local and present impression, creates a painful impression throughout our body. We find, therefore, a personal pleasure in the memory of somebody else's happiness. But in order for this memory to be often present in our minds, it must be tied to our existence, to our thought processes, and this is what happens when we are the cause of another's happiness. Then, that memory becomes part of our intimate conception of ourselves; and like that conception, it becomes a habit, and it produces in us a pleasant feeling which reaches much further than the specific pleasure that instigated it. So when we bring others a positive benefit, the pleasure we experience as a result does not depend on the nature of the pleasures they receive. But when we free someone from suffering, our pleasure, like theirs, being born out of the cessation of pain, it is even more natural that the memory we retain of it should not preserve the detail, or even the nature of the actual suffering.

Therefore, the pleasure of performing good deeds is joined by the longlasting satisfaction of having done so, a sentiment which then becomes, in some ways, general and abstract, as it is felt anew when we remember good deeds without our having to recall their particular circumstances. We have already discussed, in the first letter, this sentiment which is the most general principle of the metaphysics of the soul, just as the theory of abstract ideas is the most general principle of the metaphysics of the mind.[2] It is still the sweetest of all our sensations, that which is most similar to our moral affections, which draws the mind and delights it without pressing upon it the insatiable and voracious activity of the passions. It is the only one capable of making up for all the torments humankind is susceptible to, the only one that is always under our power, never cheating our desires but always answering them, always soothing and filling the heart, and being an insoluble tie between us and others. Happy, my dear C***, is he who always carries this sentiment deep in his soul, and dies feeling it still! Only he has truly lived!

If the sight or the idea of someone else's unhappiness gives rise in us to painful feelings, these feelings are sharper still when we are the voluntary, or even the involuntary, cause of this unhappiness. If the manner of our causing this unhappiness is completely involuntary— that is, if it cannot be attributed to our intention, thoughtlessness or carelessness—then the intensity of our painful emotion is due to its being closely tied to our memory, is more immediate, and is harder to dismiss. If by our thoughtlessness or carelessness we cause unhappiness to anybody, we will feel a greater pain because it will be linked to the idea that we could have prevented it.

An idea of this sort produces in us a very painful feeling, indeed, by contrasting the state we are in through our fault and that in which

---

2. Here Grouchy draws a contrast between the soul (realm of feelings) and mind (realm of ideas), which is derived from Locke but also Condillac.

we could otherwise have been. The thought that we could be better off makes that painful feeling stronger, for the same reason that we feel evil more strongly when it follows goodness, or that a possible good, when the imagination pictures it vividly, can be the object of regret just as much as a real one would. The fear of causing the same evil again is added to that painful feeling, producing a painful sensation that brings about the resolution to avoid any occasion that might lead to it, and is thus the inspiration for prudence. When we have done evil voluntarily, all these causes come to be, and more strongly so; and they are joined by a particular pain, that of feeling toward ourselves the unpleasant sentiment others experience at the sight of one who has hurt others.

Just as knowing that we have done something good becomes tied to our existence and makes it more pleasurable, the consciousness that we have caused some harm troubles our existence by causing us to experience feelings of regret and remorse that are upsetting, distressful, disturbing, and painful, even when the painful memory of the harm we caused is no longer distinct in our minds.[3]

Fear of remorse is enough to keep all men away from evil, either because all are at least a little acquainted with remorse, even for a small misdeed, or because imagination alone suffices to give an idea of the torments that result from remorse even to a person who has only ever done good—if indeed such a person even existed! The satisfaction that comes with good deeds and the terror of the memory of bad ones are both efficacious causes of behavior.[4] Both are universal sentiments, and they are part of the principles and grounds of human morality.

You will now easily understand, my dear C***, as I have set out the origin and nature of these sentiments, and bearing in mind what

3. See *TMS* II.2.4, p. 81.
4. See *TMS* I.3.3.8, p. 65.

you have read in the preceding letters about particular sympathy and the effects of enthusiasm on the force of habit, that they can become active, are permanent, and acquire, depending on the circumstances, a determining strength, even an irresistible force. Thus, for example, remorse for a bad deed, or even the fear of such remorse, will increase when we think of its duration, as the imagination paints a picture of the misfortunes it will generate throughout our lives. This faculty is one of the most deadly enemies of man's peace because, more insatiable than the heart, it renders him incapable of enjoyment, always carrying his thoughts beyond his possessions and capacities. But it is also one of the most efficacious causes of his happiness, as it draws to his attention the effects of vice and virtue, reminds him that he has the power to benefit and harm others, and that at the same time he can always carry within himself a sense of happiness, thus making a great part of his happiness independent of fate and helping him face death and bear all life's miseries.

Here, my dear C***, we have a distinction, already established through sentiment alone, between our actions. Some come with a pleasurable feeling and the mind is satisfied by them, while others come with pain and are followed by a sentiment that is always unpleasant, and often painful also.

But the more lasting sentiment of satisfaction or pain, which comes with the memory of the good or bad we have done to others, is necessarily altered by reflection. And it is those adjustments that lead us to the idea of moral good and evil, this first and eternal rule with its judgment which is prior to that of human laws, a rule that very few laws have sanctioned or developed, but that so many have violated, and that prejudices have stifled, and in such absurd manner! When, for instance, we give a person pleasure that will last but a short time, and will have no influence on the rest of their life, if our motivation is not that of particular sympathy, then we will receive less satisfaction than we would had we given that person pleasure that was also a lasting benefit. Perhaps we will repent, even, for having left that person in the grip of real hardship, when we only offered them temporary help, and instead of satisfaction, we will feel remorse. Here we see, therefore, the beginning of a distinction between the good deeds we do through luck and those we do through reflection, the good we are drawn to do by a particular sympathy and that we do from general sympathy.[5] When we follow a particular sympathy, we obey, in doing so, the instinct of our hearts. But if we act out of general sympathy, when we are indifferent among several possible good deeds, or cannot decide between one inspired by our inclination and another, greater deed toward which we are not inclined, we weigh the benefits to others and we choose according to that which will bring us, if not the greatest present pleasure, the more lasting satisfaction.[6]

From this point, our actions, which were before simply beneficial and humane, acquire moral goodness and beauty, and from this is born the idea of virtue—that is, *of actions that give others pleasure in a way that is sanctioned by reason.*[7]

5. Smith grounds this in resentment; Grouchy's is a much more Hobbesian moral psychology (because of the important of pleasures and pains in her account).

6. These seem like utilitarian calculations and a case can be made for describing Grouchy as a sympathetic consequentialist (see introduction, this volume). At the time she was working on the *Letters*, Grouchy was corresponding with her friend Etienne Dumont, who was working with Jeremy Bentham in London, translating his work into French. Their surviving letters show that they exchanged books and ideas, and that Grouchy had a strong interest in Bentham's work.

7. Emphasis in the original. This is reminiscent of Kant's claim in the *Anthropology*: (*Anthropology from a Pragmatic Point of View*, trans. Victor Lyle Dowdell [Carbondale and Edwardsville: Southern Illinois University Press, 1996], 7: 266, 173–174).

The ambition of a person may always be an inclination whose direction is sanctioned by reason; but the ambitious person desires, nevertheless, to be loved by others also; he needs pleasant relations with others, maintenance of his assets, and so forth. But if he is, however, passionately ambitious, then he is blind to those other purposes that his inclinations also offer to him. Consequently he ignores completely that he is hated by others or that he runs the risk of impoverishing himself through his extravagant expenses. This is foolishness (making one's partial purpose the whole of one's purpose) which even in its formal principle smacks reason right in the face.

The idea of a distinction between the moral and physical harm inflicted on someone is more difficult to grasp, but no less precise. When it happens that a small harm done to one individual would prevent a greater harm done to another, or an equal harm to many others, then if we do not inflict this small harm, we will be afflicted by the remorse of not having prevented the greater harm much more than we would have allowed had we inflicted the smaller harm. By contrast, the regret of having inflicted the lesser harm will be softened by the stronger satisfaction of having prevented the more serious harm. The same is true in relation to any pleasure we may derive from harming someone else: such pleasure will be weak and will not compensate us for the remorse that comes with inflicting this harm. In all those circumstances, we become used to consulting our reason as to what the best course of action is, and we settle on the one that will give us the greatest satisfaction afterwards, and thus we acquire the idea of moral evil—that is, of *an act that is harmful to others and which is prohibited by reason.*[8]

This definition strikes me as more accurate than the one proposed by Vauvenargues, who says that moral good and evil refer to whatever is more useful or harmful to humanity in general.[9] These two definitions are fundamentally the same, as any good or evil that reason approves or disapproves of corresponds to that which is useful or harmful to humanity. But Vauvenargues's definition is less precise and harder to grasp because it does not take into account the idea that moral good and evil can be found even in the common man.

8. Emphasis in the original. This definition moves Grouchy further from utilitarianism, in that evil is not simply defined as "an act that brings pain." In particular, it seems that for her what reason sanctions is treating people equally and what she prohibits is treating them unequally.

9. Bernier and Dawson cite Vauvenargues's *Réflexions et Maximes* (1746): "Afin qu'une chose soit regardee comme un bien par toute la societe, il faut qu'elle tende a l'avantage de toute la societe, et afin qu'on la regarde comme un mal, il faut qu'elle tende a sa ruine: voila le grand caractere du bien et du mal moral" (Bernier and Dawson, *Lettres sur la Sympathie*, 74n50). For more on Grouchy's point, see the introduction, this volume.

For ordinary reason and conscience are not enough to understand good and evil from a universal perspective. Yet it matters more than is sometimes thought, in defining moral concepts, that we should prefer those definitions that the least enlightened of men may grasp. For when it comes to uncovering the general laws ruling the human heart, the most reliable and enlightened reason is that which is the most common.

Once the idea of moral good and evil is acquired, we become quite used to distinguishing the one from the other; we can tell how doing something or, on the contrary, refraining from doing it will lead to pleasure or pain, satisfaction and remorse, without having to weigh or calculate the consequences of doing so.[10] The idea of goodness promises a private satisfaction, and the idea of evil tells us that remorse will follow, precisely because the very idea of pleasure or pain can produce a pleasing or painful sentiment, now or in the future. This is similar, in some respect, to that practice in the sciences of relying on certain methods and principles as being correct, without having to remember the evidence we have received that they are. In the same way, we obey general sentiments without thinking back to the way in which they were first formed and all that justified them.[11]

In that way also, in order to feel remorse for the harm and satisfaction for the good we have done, we do not need to retrace the consequences of those deeds in our imagination. We may no longer even have the general memory of having done something good or bad but, rather, a more abstract sentiment of good or evil doing. It may be that other sentiments come into play, depending on the

10. This is again suggestive that Grouchy adopted a form of consequentialism. See the introduction, this volume, for a discussion of her position.
11. Smith uses the language of general rules rather than general sentiments; Grouchy's analogy is novel, however.

circumstances, but they are not necessary for our conscience to act on our soul and determine, cast judgment on, or reward our actions. However, such feelings tend more often to strengthen the moral sentiment rather than weaken it. Our remorse for the harm we have caused and our satisfaction for the good we did increase, for instance, according to whether the signs of pain or pleasure they have caused are more expressive or moving, is more capable of impressing our imagination and, through it, of speaking to our conscience. Souls that are easily moved more often act on such feelings, whereas those whose sensibility is deeper and more reasoned usually act according to those more abstract and general sentiments that accompany good and evil. The former, when they do good, do so more freely, whereas the latter acts in a more orderly fashion and with more attention to justice. The former derive a stronger pleasure from it, but the latter offers a pleasure that is more influenced by reason, but also is more often mixed with a measure of self-esteem. The former have a tendency to act rashly and blindly, the latter to neglect the good because of a stubborn determination to seek the best. One could wish for the former to be more common among the large number of men who have only superiors or equals, and the former among the class—too prevalent—of those who rule and govern because of either a legitimate right or a secret power.

The greater ability for experiencing abstract and general feelings—that is, feelings that are only the consciousness of what several individual feelings have in common, like the greater ability for forming abstract and general ideas—is the greatest distinction of hearts and minds. Only those hearts capable of such feelings are truly just, for it is only those that are capable of being ruled by immutable principles. Only on the sensibility of such hearts can we rely, as they are always susceptible to being moved by general motives. Their conscience is silenced with difficulty—and it is always active. Remorse is in them less fallible and more efficacious, with all the ideas of its duties more complete. Such people especially know to fulfill these delicate duties of honesty that morality alone imposes and recognizes, and which always bring regret and the loss of feelings of happiness when they are forgotten, and display those disinterested virtues that are the fruit of a sublime need to have always the greatest and most satisfying idea of oneself.[12]

Forgetting those abstract and general sentiments, or being incapable of having them, brings about a kind of egoism, which then smothers these sentiments completely. For indeed, the culpable and mean habit of relating all objects first to oneself, and of judging them essentially from that perspective, little by little weakens the sentiments associated with good and evil. Egoism is thus insufficiently punished when it is judged to be less dangerous and blameworthy than passions, which are more harmful in appearance, such as hatred, vengefulness, and even envy. These passions are nearly always short-lived; they are rare and only ruinous to very few men, while egoism smears and tortures entire classes. Laws nearly always repress the excesses of these other passions, but egoism is as yet only weakly condemned and weakly punished by morality and opinion. Finally, these passions, it is true, do sometimes result in violent actions. If egoism does not result in such violence, it is nearly always because of the fear of being on the receiving end of the same violence. On the other hand, it will lead to all sorts of hidden injustices or oppression.[13] If these other passions make men more fearsome, egoism makes them more corrupt, because it leaves virtue no other motivation than self-esteem and offers no restraint than others' respect, an ineffectual barrier in the face of the manipulations of cunning.

12. This is a very Smithian idea: "It is a stronger love, a more powerful affection, which generally takes place upon such occasions; the love of what is honourable and noble, of the grandeur, and dignity, and superiority of our own characters" (*TMS* III.3.4, p. 158).
13. This is interesting in connection to what she says about property rights in Letter VI.

Minds that have neither strength nor breadth enough to reach general and abstract ideas, to grasp and combine their components, will never achieve great results nor, consequently, add new truths to the sphere of knowledge—and sometimes they cannot even comprehend those truths that result from calculations or extended comparisons.[14] Thus it would be in vain to attempt to convince those who cannot grasp such ideas to adopt opinions derived from them. Concerned only with trivial and isolated matters, particular and insular opinions, such a person will qualify as dangerous any system that he cannot understand, and, with his false prudence constituted as pride, he will scornfully shut himself inside his errors.

There is a scale of sorts concerning the ability to grasp abstract and general ideas, against which all minds can be measured according to their place and their relationships to each other. Those who, through reflection or a kind of instinct, have acquired the habit of always extending or generalizing their ideas never stop doing so. Those for whom this need to acquire more and greater ideas has been prevented or stifled by other passions (as is the case for most people) ordinarily remain at the same level on the scale, and they no longer, as it were, change their ideas. This is the reason why it is so difficult to enlighten men, even concerning their own true interests.[15] First, one must look for some force in their passions that is capable of renewing and extending their intelligence, which is weakened by inaction or degraded by falsehood. Then, we must make them embrace the

14. By contrast, Smith insisted that many innovations could be the product of efforts to save time by ordinary workers, even child laborers (see Adam Smith, *An Inquiry into the Nature and Causes of the Wealth of Nations*, in *The Glasgow Edition of the Works and Correspondence of Adam Smith*, ed. R. H. Campbell, A. S. Skinner, and W. B. Todd (Indianapolis, IN: Liberty Fund, 1981), 1.1.8, pp. 20–21).

15. This seems to be underlined by a theory of adaptive preferences of the kind Condorcet put forward in his paper for granting women rights of the city, and by Mary Wollstonecraft (*A Vindication of the Rights of Men, A Vindication of the Rights of Woman*, ed. Janet Todd (Oxford: Oxford University Press, 1992).

truth, either by presenting it in clever and dazzling forms that make it seductive or by captivating their reason slowly, using a logic so steady that the last step toward the conclusion is no more difficult to take than the first.

It is therefore desirable that one of the main objects of education be to provide some ease in acquiring general ideas and in experiencing those abstract and general sentiments I was telling you about.[16] But common educational practices are ordinarily very far from fulfilling this goal. The study of grammar, which comes before all others, it is true begins (when children understand it) to give a few notions of metaphysics, but the most false or at least the most incoherent ones. They then study languages by mechanically translating authors whose thoughts they rarely comprehend. The study of history nearly always comes next, but without mention of those great results that alone can make it useful, as otherwise it would be too easy for them to recognize these abuses they are taught to respect. They are brought up amid all the prejudices of pride and vanity, and these deprive them of the sentiments of those inalienable rights common to all men, of real happiness and real merit, and give them instead the notion of artificial pleasures and superiority, which, when they are desired or respected, make their mind smaller, corrupt their reason, and extinguish their conscience. Any morals they are taught nearly always consist in a few isolated precepts in no particular order, with the most insignificant duties mixed with the most sacred ones, presented in the same way and given the same importance. Only rarely does this instruction cause them to look into their own heart and to seek

---

16. Note that the discussion of the failings of the educational system is a summary of the debates on the reform of education that started before the Revolution and that was taken up first by Talleyrand and later by Condorcet; but is also very close to Wollstonecraft's (*Thoughts on the Education of Daughters* [London: J.Johnson, 1787]), which it is possible Grouchy had just read, as she alludes in a letter to Dumont to a book he sent her by an English female philosopher on that very subject, and which she greatly admired.

there those eternal and general laws that distinguish good from evil, and to listen to sentiments that praise the one and punish the other. Scientific studies are nearly always abandoned at the point where the mind, already accustomed to content itself with vague ideas and to prefer to deal with words than with the world, finds it hard to follow their methodical reasoning, is wearied even by the most obvious ones, and grasps with difficulty their general principles or is incapable of deriving new conclusions from them.

Let us therefore, my dear C***, stop reproaching nature for the lack of great men; let us not be surprised that we should know so little of the general laws of nature. How many times in one century does education succeed in giving a mind the necessary strength and rectitude to form abstract ideas? How many times has it succeeded in perfecting the mind's instinct for truth or has strengthened its propensity to pursue the truth and nothing else, to be always nourished by it? How often, on the contrary, does it not lead us astray, toward trivial and common opinions, from prejudice to prejudice, from error to error? How often, for instance, has it distorted our need to live only for useful, true, and great pleasures toward which nature directs our mind and our heart, toward the need to live only for deceitful pleasures restricted to self-love and vanity? Eh! How many virtues, talents, and lights has this mistake alone stolen from us, and each day still steals from humankind?

Chapter 9

Letter VI

The Same Subject Continued

You saw, my dear C***, that when we harm or benefit others, we experience sentiments that, joined with reflection, give us the abstract idea of moral good and evil. This idea gives birth to that of justice and injustice. And that idea differs from the first only in the following way: reason's endorsement of a just action must be guided by the idea of right—that is, a preference ordered by reason itself in favor of a person and because of which we must prefer that person's interest even when particular circumstances may make it seem weaker than somebody else's interest. Thus, a man who, in the state of nature, has taken pains to cultivate a field, to supervise its harvest, has a right to this harvest. That is, reason demands that it be his because he bought it through his labor, because by taking it away from him, and making his work useless, depriving him of what he had long looked forward to and of the possession he deserved, we hurt it more than we would if we were to deprive him of a similar harvest that just happened to be within his reach. Reason demands that we give him preference even when he does not need all his harvest while another has a real need of some harvest—and this is precisely what constitutes right. It is grounded in reason, on the necessity of general laws to rule over actions, common to all men, and makes it unnecessary for us to examine the motives and consequences of each particular act. It is also grounded in sentiment, for since the effect of injustice is more harmful for its victim than just the effects of mere harm, it must inspire in us a greater repugnance.

You might find it hard to accept at first glance, my dear C***, that in the state of nature, the man I mentioned just now, whose harvest was bigger than what he needed for his subsistence, should not be compelled by his neighbor—without its being unjust—to share the excess with a third person who did not have enough to see to his own needs. If you think about it, you will see that this man's right to his harvest comes from his labor, not his needs, and that this right came into being through the work itself, and that even if his humanity must lead him to renounce it, reason will not allow someone else to compel him to do so. You will see also that this man, if he refuses to share his returns with the poor, commits a lesser crime than the powerful neighbor who would use force to make him act benevolently. The first lacks humanity, the second violates one of the general laws that reason dictates and causes men to respect, showing that they serve the common interest, and that the good that comes from breaking those laws in a few rare particular circumstances cannot be compared to the advantages produces by their generality and inevitability.[1] If, driven by absolute necessity,[2] he who violates the right of another solely in order to satisfy this immediate need may be morally excused, this does not entail the general negation of this strict right. If it ceases to exist in this hypothetical absolute necessity, it is because, then, he

1. Although here the requirement that we should show humanity to each other seems to fade in comparison with that of respecting rights derived from reason, Grouchy believes that the former is just as important as the latter. See Letter V.
2. "Absolute necessity" refers to circumstances (famine) when property rights can be infringed legitimately. On some of the history of the so-called right of necessity, see, for example, John Salter, "Grotius and Pufendorf on the Right of Necessity," *History of Political Thought* 26, no. 2 (2005): 285–302.

who refuses the necessary subsistence is an enemy, attacking in a way the life of the person he will not help.

Perhaps this definition of *right* seems incomplete to you, as the word *preference* appears contrary to *natural equality*, which is the foundation for part of men's true rights. But this is not a real contradiction; for when equality is harmed and we must give preference to the person who is suffering because of it, we are only preferring the recovery of equality over a superiority that reason does not recognize. Thus the right that we have over everything that allows us to reach equality is justice, not indulgence.

A right such as property right is positive: it consists in a preferment grounded in reason for the enjoyment of a particular thing. A right such as liberty is in some ways negative. It only exists because of the possibility that it might be in someone's interest to threaten my liberty. In this case, it would be reasonable to defer to that person's interest—my own in preserving it—because there are no reasons why this person should hold over me a power I do not hold over him. The same is true concerning equality. If another claims a preference over me that is not grounded in reason, reason demands that I should give preference to my interest in maintaining that equality rather than give preference to his claim. This is because submitting to another's will and being inferior in any respect is a greater evil than subjugating another's will and achieving superiority is a good. The idea of moral good and evil requires us to submit the natural sentiment of sympathy to reason so that it is directed towards the more pressing interests. The ideas of justice and injustice require that we submit to reason, which is itself led by general rules, by a preference grounded in general and reasoned concerns that aim at the greatest good—that is, in a preference for rights.

Don't you see, my dear C***, that if we appeal to this precise definition of "rights," the monstrous structure of the so-called rights of the despot, the aristocrat, and the priest, and all those whose power is unsanctioned will simply collapse? These are prerogatives, which even though they banished liberty and equality from our midst, many nations, through ignorance and weakness, still describe as rights! As if reason could approve of leaving a sovereign (who may sometimes be a tyrant) unchecked, except by his remorse, the progress of the enlightenment, or the despair of his victims?[3] As if reason allowed that the merit of fathers was anything more than a prejudice in favor of children! As if it authorized a religious leader (should a true religion exist) to possess oppressive riches, and to let intolerance be the result of his ministry! Last, as if it could allow that any power originally established for the interest of those submitted to it should become a source of tyrannical privileges and impunity for its custodians! How did it come to be, however, that the sacred title of right, which has been used everywhere to hide and disguise the power of might, became a mask inscrutable for the multitude, in spite of the fact that it is in their interest to tear it off? For a long time, no doubt, those governing men calculated that they could easily master the people by keeping their reason oppressed under the weight of need; that they could enchain the great by giving them the people, and entertain their vanity with rattles;[4] and that all they had to fear was, from the former, excessive misery, and from the latter, general enlightenment.

An action that conforms to right is just; one that is contrary to right is unjust.

Just as an evil is greater if it is more unexpected, the painful sentiment brought on by injustice is stronger than that which an equal harm that was not an injustice would bring.[5] The strength of this

---

3. This is an example of the republican thought of Grouchy: she insists that what makes monarchy unacceptable is not that a particular king is bad but, rather, that he could become so, and that subjects have no way of safeguarding their freedom from the ruler's arbitrary will.

4. Grouchy uses this same image in the "Reflections on the King's Letter," published anonymously in *Le Républicain* in the summer of 1793.

5. Smith makes a similar point about the Calas case (*TMS* III.2.12, p. 140).

sentiment is increased yet by personal interest, because as each person has rights, he cannot see the rights of others violated without feeling keenly the idea that his own rights might be violated. Moreover, injustice supposes, on the part of the person committing it, either fraud or violence; and it alerts us to the presence of an enemy to be feared by all. It also produces in us an unpleasant sentiment of mistrust and fear.

The sentiment that leads us to be just is stronger than that which moves us to do good, because it comes together with the fear of a more violent remorse; but the satisfaction we derive from having acted justly may be weaker than that we derive from having directly benefited someone. The former is grounded, like the latter, on sympathy and is therefore in itself just as powerful; but its nature seems of a different kind—more serene, less active, and less enjoyable.

From the idea of rights and justice is born the idea of our obligations to others.

We are obliged to do voluntarily all that another could expect of us independently of our will, without harming our rights; such is the strict sense of obligation that is limited to the objects of an absolutely strict justice. But when we talk of the acts that we could be obliged to do by another, without violating our own rights, we are not talking of a real or physical possibility but, rather, an ideal one. So, for instance, we can say of a judge that he is obliged to judge according to what he believes to have been proven, even though it is not physically possible to force him to do so.

Our actions therefore, my dear C***, are subject to two rules, reason and justice, the latter being nothing but reason reduced to one absolute rule. We have already found, in the private satisfaction of having benefited someone, and in the remorse of having harmed them, some very powerful internal reasons for obeying these two rules. But there is yet another reason: the pleasure immediately inherent in following reason and fulfilling an obligation. I am quite certain that the existence of such sentiments is independent of the opinions of others.[6]

The first of these two sentiments would appear to have the same source as the pleasure born out of feeling our own strength. Indeed, we experience a satisfying feeling when we follow our reason, because we tell ourselves that were we to be led toward some evil by an unreasonable impulse, we could rely on our reason to correct that impulse and to avoid that evil. The greater part of what I have said (in Letter IV) relating to the pleasure of exercising our faculties, is even more completely suited here, as reason is among our faculties one of the greatest, the most useful and important. Is there a more reassuring and sweeter sentiment than that of knowing, through our very experience, that we possess such a guide, such a guardian of our happiness, securing our peace of mind! The pleasure we derive from following our reason is also made of the sentiment of our freedom, and of a sort of independence and our superiority to certain things that could potentially harm us. Thus it reassures us, and raises us in our own esteem, and satisfies the natural leaning for depending only on our own selves, a leaning that originates in the greater certainty we have of our well-being when it is in our own hands.[7]

The pleasure we find in fulfilling an obligation is closer to that of reassurance, the sweet sensation of being protected from resentment, vengeance, and hatred. The particular satisfaction that comes when we avoid a regret that would have haunted us is increased with the hope of never being subject to remorse, a delightful hope that banishes the idea of any intrinsic obstacle to our happiness.

---

6. Smith (e.g., *TMS* III.2.3, p. 114) wished to make the judgments of the impartial spectator within independent of the opinions of others and to be grounded in the love of praiseworthiness.

7. Here the appeal to self-sufficiency may be another trace of the Stoics' influence on Grouchy's thought. But it is also a feminist theme of the late eighteenth century, with Wollstonecraft's praise of independence, material, social, political, and above all intellectual.

We have reasons, therefore, not just to do something good for others but also to prefer good deeds over bad ones, and even just ones over unjust ones. These reasons are based on our natural sympathy, which itself is a consequence of our sensitivity. Until now, these reasons have not been influenced by any consideration tied to a foreign object. The morality of our actions, the idea of justice, the desire to follow it are the necessary work of sensitivity and reason. Any reasonable and sensitive being will have, regarding this, the same ideas. The limits of those ideas will be the same; they can, therefore, become the objects of exact science, as they are constant. Indeed, we can use the word *just* to mean anything we like, but any one who can reason well will have a common notion of justice.[8] Moral ideas are not arbitrary, hence their definitions can only be so insofar as they are not presented clearly or generally enough.

It was necessary to establish the first grounds, to show that our moral sentiments originated in natural and unthinking sympathy for others' suffering, that our moral thoughts originated in reflection.[9] It had to be shown, especially that assenting to a moral truth differs from assenting to a mathematical or physical truth, in that what naturally follows from such assent is a desire to behave in conformity with it, to see others do the same, fear of not conforming to it, and regret not having done so. We cannot say, however, that morality is

---

8. A "common notion" is a technical term in Stoicism taken up in the natural law tradition. It means, then, something that has a kind of axiomatic status that is widely accepted. It was given prominence in the eighteenth century by Leibniz's *Meditations on the Common Notion of Justice* (1704). But it is possible that all Grouchy here means to be saying is that with fairly minimal cognitive competence, one can have understanding of the common concept of justice.

9. The distinction between natural and moral sentiments is also very important to Smith's philosophy, but Grouchy's claim here is distinctive. On Smith's use, see María Alejandra Carrasco, "Adam Smith's Reconstruction of Practical Reason," *Review of Metaphysics* 58, no. 1 (2004): 81–116; and Eric Schliesser, "Reading Adam Smith after Darwin: On the Evolution of Propensities, Institutions, and Sentiments," *Journal of Economic Behavior & Organization* 77, no. 1 (2011): 14–22.

grounded in sentiment alone, as it is reason that teaches us what is just and unjust. But it is even less arguable that it be grounded solely in reason, as reason's judgment is nearly always preceded by and followed by a sentiment that asserts and ratifies it.[10] And it is even originally from sentiment that reason acquires moral ideas and derives principles.

Smith, recognizing that reason is incontestably the source of general ideas and morality,[11] but nonetheless finding it impossible to deduce from it the first principles of justice and injustice, concludes that these first impressions are the fruit of an immediate sentiment, and he claims that our knowledge of justice and injustice, of virtue and vice, derives in part from whether they agree with a sort of intimate sense that he assumes without defining. However, this intimate sense is not one of those first causes the existence of which we can only recognize but never explain. It is nothing but the effect of sympathy, to which we are prone because of our sensibility. I discussed the various phenomena of this sympathy, which has become a general sentiment to be awoken by the abstract ideas of good and evil and must which consequently always accompany our judgments on the morality of actions. Let us beware, my dear C***, of this dangerous tendency to posit an "internal sense," a faculty, a principle, every time we come across a fact we cannot yet explain;[12] of this philosophy that, too careless with evidence, rejects ignorance and doubt, prefers imagination when observation suffices, invents causes when it cannot discover them, and not only pulls us away from the truth but also weakens the understanding. It is this philosophy alone that created these systems, either insufficient or false in their principles, which,

---

10. Here she uses "grounded" not as a justificatory source but more as a psychological pull.
11. cf. Smith (*TMS* VII.3.2.7, p. 320), where Smith talks of reason as the source of the "general rules of morality."
12. Smith makes a similar criticism of Hutcheson at *TMS* VII.3.3.8, pp. 322–323.

aiming to explain beyond what can be known or what can only be revealed in the term of several centuries, have disfigured or weakened the power of those most useful and sacred moral truths by mixing them up with monstrous fables.[13]

It is not necessary, therefore, to look outside nature, and always far from it, for reasons to be a good person, reasons that tend to be as incomprehensible as they are independent from our direct or indirect interest. The human moral constitution is neither evil nor corrupt,[14] nor even indifferent, because it carries within itself a general reason for doing good and no reasons for doing evil.

But is that reason sufficient? This question, the most important concerning morality, deserves to be discussed carefully, especially as so far it has been broached only lightly and partially, either because those who did so wanted it answered negatively, so as to substitute morality's natural arguments, the imaginary grounds more favorable to their private interests, or because it has never been considered in isolation from the current state of civilization, calculating what it might become but, on the contrary, taking it as a constant given, or as a state nearly impossible to perfect.[15]

In order to find out whether the fear of feeling remorse for an injustice sufficiently balances out the interest one might have in committing it, one must examine this interest and what causes it. For if

13. This is an interesting claim about the significance of history, especially in the light of the fact that Grouchy relies on history much less than does Smith or Rousseau.

14. A clear rejection of the doctrine of original sin. The whole paragraph is an attack on religious authority when it comes to virtue.

15. Bernier and Dawson note here that this letter owes much to Condorcet's last work, the *Sketch of Human Progress*, and in particular its last part where he discusses the possibility of the future progress of human civilizations (Bernier and Dawson, *Lettres sur la Sympathie*, 85n58). However it might be more accurate to note in this case that the letter anticipates the *Sketch*, and that perhaps it even influenced it. Although many of Condorcet's notes for that work predate his wife's writings, they worked on the final draft together and, indeed, she prepared the edition after his death, almost certainly contributing some passages of her own (see the introduction, this volume).

we were to find that it is less the result of nature than of a few social institutions, if the fact that there were too few reasons to abstain from unjust behavior was nearly entirely the result of these institutions, then one would have to try and reform them and cease to calumniate human nature.

If to the personal interest we have in being unjust we oppose a personal interest in being just, and if the greater preponderance of the first could be attributed to vicious institutions, and that without them the second were in general nearly always equal or superior to the first, the fact that our reasons to do good are insufficient would be only the consequence of our mistakes, and not of a naturally vicious disposition.

If, at last, it could be demonstrated that the influence of our reasons for practicing virtue and following justice, an influence that would be so easily strengthened and broadened by education, is on the contrary so often weakened and defeated by it, and that the prejudices and anti-sympathetic sentiments[16] they create through habit become insurmountable obstacles, we could expect the following result. In people shaped and governed by reason, such sentiments would be efficacious in nearly all circumstances, and would only miss their mark in extremely rare cases, or in actions of little import. But we do not need, here, to prove that these reasons would always be sufficient, or that all men would infallibly be just if they had no others, but merely that they would be so more often. Indeed, the unnatural and artificial reasons for doing good in which some wish to ground morality nearly always miss their mark and are less capable, even, than those we are talking about to act with force and constancy, and in a sufficiently general manner so as to make them useful in all circumstances and sensible to all men. It is enough, therefore, to show that reason alone, united to sentiment, can lead to goodness through

16. "[L]es sentiments anti-sympathiques."

more secure, kinder, and less complicated means, subject to fewer errors and dangers, and that these means, far from demanding we sacrifice or silence any of our faculties, instead bring our moral perfection out of our intellectual one.

Let us pause here a moment, my dear C***, and see how this faculty of experiencing pleasure or pain at the thought of someone else's pleasure or pain, which is perfected with and by reason, becoming greater through reflection and enthusiasm, not only becomes for us a fertile source of delightful or cruel sentiments but also guarantees a life that is always gentle and peaceful to him who, faithful to reason and sensibility, obeys the call to do good and act justly, while he who behaves in the opposite manner is condemned to a life always painful and restless.

The first, living amid the good he has done or with the hope that he might do, always lives with an intimate sentiment of peace and safety. He can be alone with himself without feeling empty or listless, because one of the most active streams of his thinking always belongs to virtue. He is of course liable to pain, but that pain can never penetrate the sanctuary of his conscience where lives an inexhaustible satisfaction, where he can rest without boredom and without being troubled by the storms of passions, which he purifies through these delicate and generous sentiments, adding to them a happiness that is independent even of their satisfaction. Life and all its disappointments, men and their weaknesses, cannot trouble nor embitter him. He is easily satisfied with life because it gives him joys always accessible to him, that cannot be withered by habit, and that even ungratefulness cannot entirely corrupt; and because he sees men less in relation to what they could be, or what it is permissible to expect of them, than in relation to the happiness he can offer them. Thus, in his relations with them he is neither fussy nor worried, and it is by making them happy that he too finds happiness. He finds it hard to believe that someone would want to harm him, and he never fears that it should happen, and when someone does want to harm him and he is forced to acknowledge that they do, he is more saddened than he is angered. Except those for whom he has a particular sympathy, he cares little whose company he keeps, as there are unfortunates everywhere. Effortlessly (and nearly without merit) disinterested, he rarely fails to touch those he loves and to obtain from them the happiness he gives. But if that cannot happen, he is never subject to bitter regret, and he finds solace in and distraction from his sorrow in his enthusiasm for virtue.

How different the fate of he who resists his reason and sensitivity! He loses more happiness yet than he can take from others, always finding in the unpleasant feeling of his existence an insurmountable obstacle to his rest and always tormented by the need to run away from himself. The world looks to him empty and deserted because the circle of things that can distract him is small. In vain do passions momentarily trouble his disquiet. But they are not intoxicating enough to put his conscience to sleep. It is no longer in his power to make use of his faculties, and the happiness he could have drawn from this flees from that secret ill that troubles and imperiously dominates his soul. If he seeks men, he is soon brought back to that painful sentiment he sought to avoid, through his own inferiority in relation to them and by the mistrust inspired by that which he himself deserves. Far from seeing in his fellow man (as the good man did) someone who, independent of his will even, could bring about his happiness, he sees in him an enemy as soon as he thinks he is known to him, or he finds himself bound to all the calculations of concealment and trickery. He cannot peacefully enjoy the pleasure of being loved; never will he experience it, because he always feels like a usurper. Never confident of the feelings he inspires, he only expects from others the good he refuses them in proportion as he is able to cheat them. Trusting no one but himself, he cannot rest on a friend's shoulder and there enjoy peaceful and trusting leisure. For a rebel by nature, trust denies him peace, as well as the first component of any happy sentiment. Guiltier still, and more unfortunate, when tired of his own boredom and self-hatred, and too far from virtue to be enlightened or moved by it, he seeks, by dulling his reason and senses, to stifle any remorse that chanced to survive.

Chapter 10

Letter VII

The Same Subject Continued

All impulses toward injustice can be traced to four principal motivations:

Love's passion, the only pleasure that cannot be bought and which, consequently, remains separate from the love of money. We will not call it here sensual pleasure, as this expression has unfortunately become associated among corrupted beings with the coarsest of traffics.

The enticement of money, either for the sake of satisfying one's needs or in order to acquire riches as a general means of enjoyment.

The desire for ambition, sometimes compounded with pecuniary interest.

Last, the incentive of self-love, or vanity, which is often the cause and the aim of the previous two.

Let us examine first, my dear C***, how the desire for money or for something that can be bought may lead to injustice. If that desire answers to a real need, the incentive can be strong, and a person who lacks for everything, it seems, will have few scruples in behaving unjustly, especially toward a rich man, if he can be sure of doing so with impunity. But is such pressing need—so strong that it can stifle the voice of conscience and overcome it—common in societies ruled by reasonable laws?

Let us suppose that laws should no longer support wealth inequality; then, even if justice and humanity were to be satisfied, cupidity, which takes more time and effort to eradicate, may persist. However, is it not likely that the natural inequality caused by differences in behavior, degrees of intelligence, or the greater or lesser fecundity of families would result in the random distribution of three-quarters of resources and an equal distribution of the rest? Let us imagine, for instance, a country of six million families and a land income of twelve hundred million *livres*: each family would have two hundred *livres* in annuity from the land.[1] Even supposing that natural inequality absorbs three-quarters of that sum on behalf of the rich, wouldn't fifty *livres* remain for each family? Take a look at our peasantry, my dear C***, and ask yourself whether among those who have an income of fifty *livres*, how many are reduced to a pressing need. It is well known, on the contrary, that as soon as they own two or three acres of crop, they earn a reputation for being well-off, and the average worth of two or three acres of the best soil for wheat is around fifty *livres*.

You will be fully convinced that this hypothesis, the grounds for which are generally accepted, is not an exaggeration if you observe that among these six million families, there will be a large number who, because they engage in industrial or commercial pursuits, will have no interest in keeping their share of the land and might in some case divest themselves of it in order to pursue other activities or speculations more advantageously.[2]

---

1. Bernier and Dawson (*Lettres sur la Sympathies*) refer here to Condorcet's *Sketch* and to "Social Mathematics." It might be better to refer to his *Commerce des Blés*.
2. Empirically, this is a rejection of physiocracy influenced not only by Smith but also by Condorcet's erstwhile superior in the ministry of finances, Turgot.

The kind of pressing need that is nearly always stronger than fear of revenge or remorse can also occur in the working classes, either because of a want of wage or because of a temporary mismatch of wage with the necessities of life—most common among these people. For agriculture is, after all, the most productive of all professions for individuals, while for states, it is the unique source of real and lasting wealth.

But now we have conclusive evidence that lack of wages or insufficient wages were caused nearly entirely by prohibitive laws hampering commerce and industry.[3] Those laws at the same time were harming the well-being of all by consolidating, little by little in the hands of a few, wealth that then became a means of oppression and that otherwise, through the free movement of interests, would have remained if not equal at least common to all. The unequal distribution of the tax burden at last overwhelmed the lower class who, with no property and no liberty, were reduced to rely on fraud and would cheat remorselessly because conscience cannot survive when it is in chains. The incentive to behave unjustly, when it is based on need, is therefore extremely rare in the absence of bad laws; even when they are present, this incentive is weak, its effects are the least widely spread, and it is to be feared the least.[4]

You will notice, my dear C***, that the incentive to behave unjustly for the sake of wealth acquisition presupposes the possibility that one might succeed. But this possibility is still, in many respects, a product of the law. Were the law clear, it would warn all equally; were it just, it would admit of no exception; were it exact, it would leave no opening for corruption and bad faith. Were civil administration

---

3. This is probably a reference to the ideas developed in Condorcet's *Commerce des Blés* (1776); see Anne-Robert-Jacques Turgot, *Reflections on the Formation and the Distribution of Riches*, trans. William J. Ashley (New York: Macmillan, 1898); and Smith's *Wealth of Nations*.

4. These paragraphs comment show Grouchy to be a political economist and proto public-choice theorist.

everywhere not to interfere in so many activities that should be left to progress according to nature, it would not leave an opening for arbitrary power—less dangerous, perhaps, for its exercise than for all that is allowed for the sake of its gain and preservation. Finally, if laws alone ruled everywhere, if we feared them alone instead of also men and classes, then the only unjust way of acquiring more than we need would be through theft, in the real sense of the word.[5] It is thus against the temptation to steal that we ought to measure the strength of the remorse that follows an injustice, and not against the temptation to commit those furtive injustices that are encouraged by age-old example and are almost authorized by the silence or, rather, the moral failure of laws. These laws, which ought to supplement citizens' conscience, are all too often oppressive chains instead. At best, they occasionally serve as the very last obstacle to wickedness. But supposing we had reasonable laws, the temptation to steal in order to increase one's pleasures would be much weakened by the inconvenience that acting on that temptation would cause, so that it would be in fact quite rare. Our conscience then need only resist minor thefts, which are proportionately less common and less powerful in their attraction.

Social institutions are even more to blame for the desire to act unjustly, which derives from vanity and ambition. They alone are responsible for the fact that man is dominated by man rather than by laws; that a great appointment is anything other than one which it is difficult to fill; that the personal reward for filling it is anything other than the honor of having done it well, or glory, if it is such as to allow for the display of great talents; that titles other than services rendered and public esteem are needed to obtain it; or that there are other means for achieving it than being judged worthy of it. It is those social institutions alone which for every class make it the case

5. Here Grouchy is talking of the rule of law.

that the road to fortune is one of intrigue and artfulness, conspiracy and corruption; they disconnect ambition from the love of glory, which would ennoble it and purify its ways.[6] It is those social institutions, by sanctioning hereditary rights (nearly always first-generation abuses) that enable presumptuous mediocrity to rise, infallibly and tyrannically—for all such promotion becomes tyrannical if it is not established and limited by the general interest. If in all appointments one were bound by the law and forced to act according to it, if all appointments were granted by a general choice and a free election, our conscience would only rarely need to resist the sort of motivation that leads to crime or injustices inspired by ambition. Morality would no longer need to concern itself with that laxity of character and weakness of opinions, the art of courting vices and vanity, and all these corrupting means that are too often necessary for success and which intangibly undermine all the foundations of virtue.

The sort of vanity that is tied to nonpersonal qualities is obviously the work of bad social institutions, since it is only through such institutions that those qualities exist, having been adopted without good reason and always given in preference to local and particular interests over general ones. Meanwhile, pride derived from personal advantages can only become dangerous and lead to criminal acts when the general opinion, wrongly influenced by institutions, grants an exaggerated worth to frivolous traits. It is only in countries where there are courts, grandees, and ruinous fortunes, and where favor is the measure of preferment, that people are vain and passionate about their looks, as well as prone to jealousy and hatred because of them. And in such places, good looks can lead to anything, even sometimes to revolutions.[7] And then, even

---

6. See *TMS* VII.2.4.9, p. 310.
7. This connects back to her early treatment of good looks and demagogues. (It's also a trope about Alcibiades, who was Socrates's lover.)

lower-class men, who cannot hope to achieve such brilliant success, admire and envy others their positions; they are excited by the tales they hear of them, just as in Rome the meanest soldiers who could not aspire to the honors of a Triumph came back from the celebrations drunk on the frenzy of conquest.

The same is true of vanity derived from wits and talent. It only becomes dangerous when the people, seduced by charlatans and hypocrites, grant them the esteem and rewards that by right belong only to real worth. But should all vicious institutions be abolished from one end of the earth to the other; should there be only necessary and reasonable laws; and should arbitrary power which, forcing its victims to destitution and servitude reduces them to ignorance and credulity, disappear for ever, human reason will emerge from its chains still healthy and vigorous, and will prevail in all classes and shape public opinion. No longer will fake talents seduce opinion and no longer will vices in disguise dare to show themselves at its tribunals. This bad faith and base jealousy—about which we asked if they could be countered by conscience—are not even aimed at achieving glory. True glory cannot be contested, and is only disputed in ways that are fit for obtaining it.[8] Injustice can only take away the outward signs of glory. Therefore, when ambition and vanity put obstacles in the way of our conscience, the unique cause of this is the actual order of society wherever government is not grounded in the natural rights of men.[9] But in a well-ordered society, conscience will nearly always suffice to repress these obstacles, as ambition and

8. On the significance of "true glory" in Rousseau and Smith, see Ryan Patrick Hanley, "Commerce and Corruption: Rousseau's Diagnosis and Adam Smith's Cure," *European Journal of Political Theory* 7, no. 2 (2008): 137–158.

9. The (1789) French "Declaration of the Rights of Man" approved by the National Assembly of France, August 26, 1789, articulates a list of "natural, unalienable, and sacred rights." Presumably Grouchy has in mind a similar list.

vanity—were they to acquire such strength—would be in agreement with reason and justice.[10]

It is again these vicious institutions that we must hold responsible for acts contrary to morals which are motivated by love.

We do not mean here by love this tender and deep sentiment, often generous and always delicate, whose first desire is always to love, its first ambition, the sweetness of being loved, its first care, the happiness and peace of its object; which attaches a greater prize to possession than to enjoyment, knows not how to pretend nor to cheat, wants to receive, give, and deserve only through the heart, and knows no pleasure except that which it itself chooses. Such passion is not common, because it supposes mutual sympathy, difficult to find and more difficult yet to recognize; a generous character; and a rare strength of sensitivity that is nearly always accompanied by some superior qualities. Such passion does not often lead to injustice, for such is its character and its course: it is a reciprocal devotion that inspires on both sides sacrifices, and yet it does not allow from either anything really harmful; it is an involuntary forgetting of oneself in order to be transported into the existence and happiness of the loved one. Such sentiments, lasting and fine, nearly always surmount their obstacles peacefully, and their generosity and disinterestedness ordinarily make them judge themselves as severely as conscience would.

Injustice, therefore, can only be motivated here by the desire to possess, or to have possessed this or that woman. Let us now separate from this desire whatever strength society has added to it by exciting pride and vanity through its vicious institutions. We will first see that the inequality created by laws,[11] and which will persist long after

---

10. A "well-ordered society" is the counterfactual institution in which preferences are properly cultivated and incentives are properly aligned toward virtue.

11. Smith thinks that inequality is the first cause of laws, but then the rich and powerful bend the laws in their own favor (*Wealth of Nations* 5.1.a.15, 697ff.).

them, is alone responsible for the existence of an idle class for whom gallantry is an occupation, an amusement, and a game. This inequality alone is responsible for making it easy to sacrifice victims to such passion, and it makes it the instrument and accomplice of ambition and cupidity. Let us suppose next that this same inequality, and the laws made to sustain it, were no longer reducing most marriages to nothing but conventions and pacts between fortunes, so quickly concluded that it becomes apparent only long afterward whether personal preferences were met, and where the price of love is fixed at the same time as the dowry is calculated, without knowing if it is possible to love, and especially to love each other. Let us suppose at last that man would stop imposing on his fickle heart, and his will, which is even more changeable, indissoluble ties that are incompatible with his nature, whose flexibility and proud independence can only be fixed by a habitual sentiment of freedom. Let us suppose that divorce were to be allowed for all people. Let us suppose even that, as in Rome, for the sake of human weakness and the more lasting needs of one sex, it were possible to form temporary unions that the law would not repudiate but, rather, would set the conditions for.[12] From then on we will see that most unjust acts committed in the name of love (or, rather, the degradation of love) will no longer be called for. This passion will lose, through the ease of satisfaction, that dangerous strength it acquired from the obstacles it encountered. Too long has society prevented unions based on mutual taste and has set up walls between the two sexes (under the pretext of protecting virtue) such as made it nearly impossible for hearts and souls to come to know each other, as is necessary for the creation of virtuous and lasting unions. Too long has it excited and absorbed the vanity of men for the corruption of women; made it harder to experience pleasure together

12. Cf. Charles de Montesquieu, *The Spirit of the Laws*, ed. Anne M. Cohler, Basia C. Miller, and Harold S. Stone (Cambridge: Cambridge University Press, 1989), 430–431.

with feeling; and spread shame beyond what is really deserved, such as the uncertain estate of children, the violation of a formal promise, reviling indulgences, or an ease that indicates weakness and the lack of power over oneself. It is therefore society, through all these abuses, that gave birth to dangerous and corrupt passions that are not love and that made love such a rarity.

I have considered these passions here almost entirely in relation to men, but it would be easy to apply everything I said about men on this topic to women and to justify the opinion of a philosopher wiser even than he is famous: "The sins of women are the works of men, just as the vices of the people are the crime of their tyrants."[13]

You have just seen, my dear C***, how the vices of social institutions are partly responsible for the growth of the various reasons we have to behave unjustly. But it is not only by giving more strength to these reasons that they weaken the power of our conscience to resist it; they also weaken it by habitually resisting it.[14] Indeed, such reasons as we might have to act unjustly, empowered more yet by the faults of our social framework, have made man determined to do evil more often than his conscience has been able to prevent it. From then on, the influence of conscience is weakened either by habitual disregard for its warnings or by its habitual violation. For being habituated to evil, or habitually exposed to it, indirectly diminishes remorse and the fear of exposing oneself to it, except in the case of strong souls whose

---

13. This is a misquoted and out of context reference to Condorcet's "Eloge d'Hunter," in *Oeuvres Complètes de Condorcet*, ed. Sophie de Grouchy, Pierre George Cabanis, and Dominique Joseph Garat (Paris and Brunswick: Henrichs, 1804), Tome II, p. 443. In the context of Letter VII, it suggests that, like Mary Wollstonecraft, Grouchy believed that women's moral failures were to be blamed on the fact that they were dominated by men and by bad laws and institutions. This is the only remark in the *Letters* that suggest an openly feminist agenda. (We thank Stefan Heßbrüggen for directing us to the source of this passage.)

14. There is a lot throughout the *Letters* on the role of habituation in morality. This suggests that Grouchy's ethical theory was influenced at least in part by Aristotelian virtue ethics. On this, see Sandrine Bergès, *A Feminist Perspective on Virtue Ethics* (London: Palgrave Macmillan, 2014), 84–108.

vigorous sentiments of justice and goodness cannot be corrupted. I say that the habitual sight of evil diminishes remorse *indirectly* because we have a natural tendency to rid ourselves of any painful feeling; and a person tormented by remorse will strive to move way from all the ideas that keep that remorse alive, and to surround himself instead with all the objects that might lighten its weight. Vicious institutions now finish what they started, for they provide that person with the means of long deceiving his own heart. They even give him permission to look upon the evil of which they are the source and for which they then become the excuse, as inevitable, necessary, politically indifferent, or even useful. In any case, habit itself will dull any sentiment because pain, like pleasure (especially when they are not very lively), is always made greater through a comparison with a near and different state, and because the starting point of pain or pleasure is part of the intensity of the sentiment it gives us. The same is true of the man who is but the habitual witness of injustice. That injustice will grow less great in his eyes if he does not possess a strong spirit which would not lend itself to the excuses of vice, and this powerful and virile sensibility which cannot be misled nor corrupted, and which can sustain indignation for a long time without being too painfully fatigued.

As vice becomes more common, it achieves more brilliant, more visible, and greater success, and the hope of drawing from such success the means for more daring and greater projects yet excites a true interest in doing evil. The financial speculator[15] who carries out a small fraud in order to gain fifty Louis, has in his sight the practiced Croesus who made millions from a similar deal. His cupidity is not

---

15. The *agioteurs*, or financial speculators, were much reviled during the period preceding the Revolution, and were blamed for the economic crash and the resulting famine. (Smith was also critical of such "projectors" and even proposed controls on finance to prevent their actions.)

limited to a few coins; grasping enthusiastically toward the time when he too will have piles of gold, his conscience is already corrupted.

The power, therefore, of an ordinary conscience together with reasonable laws would suffice for man to be just and good. But since social institutions have, in most countries, more often degraded nature than perfected it, and since he receives from them false and incomplete moral opinions, as well as passions more dangerous than the ones he has by nature, and since their effects destroy the justice and original strength of his conscience, in order to stay in the path of virtue, he needs that strength and powerful light that nature so rarely gives out, and that without it can only be acquired in deep and reflected meditation.

Chapter 11

Letter VIII

You saw, my dear C*, how impulses toward injustice were magnified and multiplied by vicious institutions. Far from guarding man against his own weakness, often they would take advantage of it in order to corrupt him, choosing means most likely to seduce the minority that would benefit from such corruption, and that were most capable of subduing the majority that would suffer from it. Having obstructed men for centuries in the exercise of their natural rights, these institutions led them from adversity to stupid and credulous blindness, which caused them to accept, as a law of necessity, the chains they had become incapable of seeing or breaking. It will not be difficult to show that reasonable laws can both increase the personal desire to be just and strengthen the power of conscience, even toward such objects as governed and punished by conscience alone.

Actions contrary to justice fall under two categories. Some are real crimes punishable by law. Others, either because they are less significant or because they are more difficult to secure a conviction for, do not fall under the law. In all societies where crimes are punishable by laws, and the established sentences appear to be at least as strong as they need be to deter those from committing such crimes, the effect of such sentences is nonetheless incomplete, and people complain that the laws are not sufficient in themselves.

However, we have not paid sufficient attention to what a small number of philosophers have been saying in the last few years. I will not hesitate to repeat it here, for truths must be told not only until they are adopted by every enlightened person but also until all those who defend the abuses they proscribe are silenced. The prevention of crime is less the effect of the intensity of a sentence than of its certainty; and extreme severity almost always results in impunity. Indeed, a humane man will not denounce a servant who stole from him if the sentence awaiting that servant is death.[1] The same quality almost always prevents one from denouncing small thefts that, although less severely punished, are still disproportionately punished. If, on the contrary, minor crimes were punished only by corrective sentences informed by and essentially punished through public opinion,[2] and if for all ordinary offenses and the least wrongdoings we did not break in an instant all the ties that attached the offender to society (by taking his life or covering him with permanent disgrace)—that is, the last safeguard between him and a life of crime—then all would make it a duty, for the sake of common interest, to denounce criminals. We would be less indulgent, even, were it not for the fact that need reduces people to a dulled state that excuses their crimes.[3] Criminal laws, through their severity, and civil laws, because they favor inequality, are therefore the cause of impunity for lesser crimes. And they can also be considered the cause of greater

1. Cf. *TMS* 2.2.3.10, p. 90.
2. Smith thought that for the working poor, the anonymity of urban life made this impractical (*Wealth of Nations* V.i.g.12, pp 795–796), and so required religious affiliation. But Grouchy anticipates Mill in embracing the "moral coercion of public opinion" to regulate social life. Cf. *On Liberty* I, in John Stuart Mill. *On Liberty and Other Essays*, ed. John Gray (Oxford: Oxford University Press, 1998), 14.
3. By contrast, Smith thinks that repetitive labor created a dulled state (see the "torpor of mind," *Wealth of Nations* V.i.f.50, p. 782) for which public education and enlightenment were an adequate response. If hunger and need reduce the cognitive ability presupposed in prudential and moral functioning, then the legislator who aims at virtue must ensure that people's needs are met. This is another argument for Grouchy's egalitarian tendencies.

crimes, since it is the impunity of the former that inspires the confidence needed to commit the latter.

In order for the fear of a sentence to be effective and beneficial, that sentence must not outrage. Its justice must be perceptible to average reason, and it must especially awaken the conscience at the same time as it punishes its silence and slumber. But this will not be so if sentences are too strong and, instead of inspiring horror against crime, appear barbarous and unjust themselves;[4] if they do not punish the injustices committed by the rich against the poor; if, when these injustices are not subject to sentences, the laws do not prevent them in other ways; if a judge can arbitrarily harden or soften a sentence; if there are privileges, hereditary, personal, or local, that offer a legal loophole, direct or indirect. Then the people will be tempted to see criminal laws as made against them and in favor of the rich, as the result of an association designed to oppress them. Then they will hate more and they will fear these laws that no longer inform their conscience, because they outrage their reason and this hatred is enough to overcome fear in strong souls and in all those made bitter by the joint feeling of injustice and need.

The laws that favor inequality of fortunes, as well as all the disadvantages I have already pointed out to you, have the further disadvantage of multiplying those who have nothing to lose. A man of property not only feels more strongly the justice of respecting that which belongs to others but also is restrained by the fear of losing his own property, by that of retaliation, and by the necessity of repaying at least the value of what he has stolen. Hope of restitution increases the desire to prosecute him, so that he is more worried about exposing himself to the least suspicion, and having to pay for a difficult and expensive defense. Last, if the vices of social institutions did not leave

---

4. The barbarism of European legal practices echoes the great theme of Beccaria's *On Crimes and Punishments*.

the door open for the kind of rogueries that are difficult to prove, impossible to prosecute, and sometimes dangerous even to complain about, there would be fewer people reduced to straightforward theft. By preserving their natural rights, the social order would put men in the best position to bring about mutual respect, and those rights would then be guaranteed by each person's interest in their own happiness and tranquillity, even more than it would by the law.

You see therefore, my dear C***, that social institutions are still rather far from having achieved the degree of utility one could draw from criminal law. But for this to be the case, people must be able to see those in charge of the execution of the law, of arresting the guilty and condemning them, not as the masters of the law but only as its defenders and its friends.

Having thus described what criminal laws could achieve, philosophers took the liberty of attacking such laws that bring more abuse than benefits. This indictment, ordered by all those who were not accused, and justified by all too many injustices, nonetheless earned those who undertook it the name (truly more honorable than injurious) of dangerous *novatores*.[5] But when they demanded laws from which the guilty could not escape, and from which the innocent should not fear, they were asking for just laws. When they demanded less severe laws, they demonstrated that severity could be as dangerous as it could be unjust. When they considered that reason and common utility were the natural and absolute judges of social institutions, it was because these were the only general and infallible rules.

We must therefore cease to slander philosophers, try and silence them, or maintain that the use of reason is dangerous and that reason approves of everything that is sanctioned by the past. Another reproach made to them, which is as serious in appearance as it is

---

5. In early modern philosophy, the *novatores* were those who offered new science as distinct from scholastic philosophy.

ridiculous in fact, is to claim that they wish to substitute the breaking wheel and the scaffold for the true grounds of morality, and especially for supernatural incentives for justice.[6] Those who are accused of wanting to govern through such barbaric means (should we forget?) are the very same individuals who asked that laws be milder, so as to increase their irrevocability and efficacy, and who demanded that justice and reason alone determine which sentences are proportionate to which crimes. Cruel laws backed by supernatural incentives have failed until now to keep men from criminal activities.[7] Given that, we cannot accuse of slandering human nature those who have said that milder and better organized laws, combining their strength with that of reason and conscience, would have more power to prevent crime. Are there any countries where better and more common use of supernatural incentives dispenses with punishment? Did history ever know a people who, governed by such motives, was neither barbaric nor corrupt? Let the apologists of such motives offer them as a great hope and consolation, sometimes sweet and sometimes useful, to the unfortunate man for whom the sentiment of his own virtue and courage cannot suffice;[8] but let them no longer brag that they elevate human nature at the same time as they degrade it by offering it an artificial and imaginary greatness while reviling its greatest and most noble attributes, *reason* and *conscience*. Let them no longer accuse conscience of insufficiency while it is they who make it so by

6. The breaking wheel, also known as Catherine wheel was a torture practiced on thieves and highway robbers which consisted of breaking the limbs of the victim while they were tied on a slowly rowling cartwheel.

7. Theists often argued that theism was socially necessary because if supernatural incentives disappeared, people would not have an incentive to be moral or live according to the law. This is a debate associated with Bayle's interpretation of Spinoza (see also Voltaire's essay on atheism in John Morley, *The Works of Voltaire: A Contemporary Version*, trans. William F. Fleming (New York: E.R. DuMont, 1901), 3:109.

8. See *TMS* III.2.11, pp. 120–121.

establishing, on the ruins of reason, a foreign power that can only rule among their discord.

At this point, my dear C***, you might ask how we might motivate a man who has nothing to lose so as to respect others' property. This question need not be so difficult if we only think about it. First, considering an artisan or an established farmer who subsists only through his work, he will have a greater incentive to respect others' property either because, if not, he would soon cease to be employed or because, even though he has no reliable funds to ensure his subsistence, he nonetheless possesses some clothing, animals, food, and furniture, and the poorer he is, the more he will fear to lose these last resources. If he is affluent, the fear of being stolen from will be strengthened by greed, however. If he is indigent, it will correspond proportionately to his needs. Moreover, the general utility that leads one to respect others' property is noticeable as soon as all can hope to possess something (and as I demonstrated earlier, in a well-governed country, nearly all inhabitants would have some small property). For the worker who has nothing can hope to acquire, in his prime, what he will need in his old age for his subsistence. But the very instant he ceases to respect others' property, he loses this hope, which is so dear and necessary, yet often unacknowledged by those who have not witnessed closely the lives of those unfortunates, forced each day to check their needs against their strength, and who cannot imagine any other happiness than a life in which they do not have to work, or to have at least a life free of worry.

Supposing that thefts occur only regarding what is strictly necessary in order to preserve one's life when it is being threatened by absolute need; morality might look upon that with indulgence. But it will nonetheless be the least useful and the most dangerous solution, for as long as bad laws do not greatly increase needs and accidents, one will always benefit more from legitimate and peaceful solutions. Let us only remove the extreme inequality that puts the poor too far from the rich to be known by them, and the rich too far from the poor to see them, and to let the voice of humanity reach their hearts; then unexpected misfortunes will become rarer and will certainly be mended. Take away from all the small tyrants their desolating scepter; make these heaps of gold disappear, the smallest and least illegitimate of which probably has, in secret, a thousand victims to its name; let man no longer be elevated above man in such a way that he no longer sees his duties next to his interest; and then theft and fraud will become rare enough that the greatest danger and most dreaded punishment will be their actions being made public.

Concerning unjust acts that do not fall under criminal law, we can observe that each person is keen to obtain the trust of others by achieving a reputation for probity and virtue. We prefer our farmer to be an honest man, our servant to be faithful; we prefer a craftsman who is known for his probity over one whose honesty is questionable. That this is not an efficient means of gaining trust in our societies is because a great portion of social advantages is acquired independently of general trust. This is because a large number of institutions that were established, apparently, for reasons of utility and have been preserved as if they were sacred prerogatives and properties, exempt civilized man from virtues that would be necessary even for a savage man who wished to live peacefully with his fellow men. It is because nearly everywhere, the prominence of vanity replaces the rights drawn from true merit and stifles the sentiment that accompanies it. It is because multiple obscure laws, rules, and so on make it impossible to recognize probity, or allow its reputation to be arrogated. It is because religious hypocrisy offers reliable means of gaining social advantages. It is because, under the cover of all abuses, a guilty and skillful prudence may obtain them, without even having to hide or pretend. It is because the extreme inequality of fortunes, and the great distance there is between one class and the other, renders men strangers to each other. Virtues cannot recognize each other unless they be placed, by chance, at the same level. The powerful man and the worker in his employ are too far removed from each other to be able judge one another. And because their respective duties seem to get lost in the distance between them, the one may oppress the other nearly without remorse, while the other will in turn cheat him with impunity, even believing that he is in this way bringing justice to himself. The destitution of a large class of people, the sentiment of mistrust and cupidity that comes from it and leads them to cheat, makes it all the more impossible for them to be particular about the honesty of a man they buy from or sell to. Thus in all social relations, a large number of vicious institutions that, on the one hand, abused power and, on the other, took away natural rights have isolated men from each other, making probity and justice useless and alien to them by annihilating all their advantages and any reasons to act on them.

Thus, these institutions that were meant to complete human happiness have instead long degraded and corrupted it, perhaps because until now we had only sought to use them in order to perfect nature by forgetting nature itself.

Not only did the errors of social institutions make the accomplishment of the most sacred duties indifferent to men—and only granted the full strength of the desire to fulfill them to a small number of sensitive beings, who find a necessary happiness in doing so and whose attraction to virtue cannot be erased—but also, by creating artificial needs, these institutions weakened one of the most powerful motivations for an honest life: the enjoyment of domestic peace. There, by offering exaggerated rewards, which are unjust and intoxicating honors, these institutions excited self-love until it became a dominating passion—a passion capable of stifling the most powerful and the most delicate sentiments. Here they misled it, blinded it by attaching such value on places and fortunes of birth as belong only to great actions and virtues. In all classes and in all passions, these institutions added to the first and real existence of each person an imaginary perceived existence, the needs of which were greater, more insatiable, and more inconstant, and whose pleasures were inevitably followed by disgust. A man shaped in this way could no longer be made happy or unhappy by need, by the good or bad use of his faculties, by whether or not he was in possession of their objects. No longer did he judge, act, or enjoy according to his own thoughts and sentiments. He is fettered by unjust laws, a child of fortune or drawn by her to all the abuses born of such laws, blinded and weakened by interest, nearly always in opposition to the voice of reason and humanity; he is able to satisfy his most audacious expectations, without needing to justify them through real merit, and his most corrupt passions, without being called to remorse by universal scorn. As soon as such a man could live above his needs, placed in the circle of vanity, the opinion of others, now the toy of the countless prejudices that were previously his obstacles, he becomes the measure of his conscience, the necessary sanction of his pleasures, and the first condition of his happiness.[9]

No doubt, my dear C***, this picture strikes you as an exaggeration. Devoted, without choice or effort, to your work and your affections, the habitual sentiment of reason and virtue, perhaps places you too far from men to perceive all their faults, or at least to recognize their deep roots. However, is there a society man who, looking at himself in good faith, will not find in himself the main outlines of that picture? Is there a man of the world (no matter how little invested he is in society) who in the choices he makes in his domestic and personal life, his fortune, pleasures, tastes, and even affections, is not led (by the indirect but nonetheless very real effect of our institutions)

9. Here Grouchy may be following Rousseau, who argued that luxuries corrupted the character. This claim is also made in French economic writings of the time (Condorcet and Turgot). However, we may also trace the plea for simple pleasures to the influence of ancient philosophers, such as Plato (*Gorgias, Republic*) or Marcus Aurelius.

to sacrifice to vanity that which was due to his true happiness? Where is he who, true to reason and nature, prefers the real pleasures to be found in peace and domestic virtue to those seductive pleasures of pride—that will, through habit, make us lose sight of our need, taste, or appreciation for other people? Where is he who is never carried away by all the inventions of idleness and corruption that relieve us of the weight of our own existence—a weight that soon becomes hard to bear when virtue is not part of the all-consuming charm of passions and to the arid pleasures of the intellect? Where is he, who always preserves part of his soul for the enjoyment of himself, in order to enjoy the sentiments of nature with all the indulgence and reflection they draw their sweetness and power from? Where is the man who, amid institutions, prejudices, and manners, the effect of which is to tie sensitivity to pride, still has a need for hidden and simple pleasure, for being secure at home in a reciprocal friendship, in the delicious peace of trust, goodwill, and unending indulgence, and who still finds some attraction in those sweet sentiments that passion and vanity scorn, but that nonetheless may be the frame of happiness, the only one that time does not use or let go? Where is he who, instead of seeking always far from nature a new way of enjoying or abusing of its gifts, finds each day a new pleasure in changing around him all the ties of duty and servitude into relations of charity, good faith, and kindness, and with his domestic gods creates a sanctuary where the happiness owed him forces him to partake with delight in his own existence? Private and comforting pleasures, entwined with peace and secret virtues! True and moving pleasures, never leaving the heart you once touched! You, that the tyrannical scepter of vanity always draws us away from, and that through its seductive magic we can no longer see except under the dark colors of duty, boredom, uniformity. . . Unhappy is he who disdains or abandons you! Unhappy, especially, the sex who one moment is gifted by nature with its brightest gifts, but for whom nature soon turns into a cruel mother. He must not neglect or ignore you, for he will spend half his life with you, and (if it is possible) forget that enchanted cup that the hand of time spills for him in the middle of their journey![10]

10. This is only the second reference to women in the *Letters*. But it is perhaps significant that it should be at the end of the text. In her edition of Condorcet's *Sketches*, Grouchy's added paragraphs on women and families are positioned at the beginning and the end of the text, thereby framing the argument. This may be a tactic for bringing women into philosophical debates without being obvious about it. See Bergès, "Family, Gender, and Progress" for a discussion of this.

GLOSSARY

NOTE

Grouchy's terminology is much indebted to Locke's psychology and his philosophical vocabulary. At times her uses are indebted to eighteenth-century developments and revisions of Locke primarily due to work by Condillac, Hume, and Rousseau; sometimes her uses seem original to her.

The glossary is meant to facilitate understanding for readers who may be confused by eighteenth-century technical terminology. Sometimes we offer multiple meanings of a particular term; in general, Grouchy's context of use helps disambiguate which term is the pertinent.*

Abstraction (or abstract idea): A general idea that stands for all the objects of that kind. "Abstraction" refers to the process whereby an idea of a determinate object is stripped of features that would indicate it exists in a particular time or moment.

An abstract or general feeling: A feeling that stands for what all the feelings of a particular kind have in common.

Emotion: A feeling connected to or stirred in the body.

Enthusiasm: An individual's overconfident set of assumptions or commitments about a situation or person.

Generosity: The disposition to enjoy another's happiness.

Humanity: Depending on context, it is either (i) a moral category that encompasses all human beings; or (ii) a feeling that involves this moral category; or (iii) a comportment toward others. Having the feeling of humanity presupposes fellow feeling with the physical suffering of others; this begins, thus, as a kind of generalized moral pity, but it can be cultivated into different feeling. The comportment presupposes the disposition to reflect and to show compassion to others.

Idea: A mental object produced by sensation or reflection.

Imagination: A mental capacity, or faculty, that operates on images. These can be images of reality, but need not be so.

Impression: Locke uses this term to refer to all perceptions. Not unlike Hume, Grouchy generally uses it more narrowly, in contrast to ideas or sensations, and then it refers to an original perception. But she follows Rousseau in distinguishing between general and local impressions:

General impression: A perception felt diffused through our body.

Local impression: A perception felt in a particular organ.

Moral (as opposed to "physical"): Depending on context, this can either mean "social" or "mental" (in the sense of "psychological"):

Moral idea: Idea about society.

Moral pain: Mental (or psychological) suffering.

Moral sentiment: Social (or cultivated) feeling.

Moral sensibility: The capacity to feel or apprehend another's psychological feelings.

Moral sympathy: The (disposition to) fellow-feel with the psychological pains or pleasures of another person.

Passion: A feeling (or emotion) that stirs the mind, or is experienced by the mind as well as the body.

Physiognomy: Thought to be a promising science in the eighteenth century, in which a person's face or appearance is used to evaluate character.

Pity: Concern for a person without fellow feeling. (Of course, pity can also accompany compassion.)

Reflection (or reflexion): A technical term in Lockean psychology. It is a mental mechanism akin to sensation that is a source of experience. The material the mechanism works with (or reflects) is always internal to the mind.

Sensation: The mechanism by which we have experience of external objects (through the senses).

Sensitivity/sensibility: A property of matter that facilitates our capacity to experience the world through the senses. For Grouchy, it's a disposition that can be cultivated and improved.

Sentiment: A feeling accompanied by a thought. So, in particular, it is any thought prompted by a passion:

Natural sentiment: An uncultivated feeling accompanied by a thought.

Moral sentiment: A cultivated or social feeling accompanied by a thought.

Soul: Generally, this means the mind of a person. Grouchy seems to be a materialist or functionalist, so there is no need to infer that she embraces an immortal or immaterial substance. Sometimes she uses "soul" to refer to the character of a person. She sometimes uses *esprit*, which also means "mind," but tends to refer to a person's intellectual, rather than emotional functions.

Sympathy: A disposition to fellow feeling with others:

General sympathy: Fellow feeling with the pain (or pleasures) of a class of human beings (or even mankind).

Personal sympathy: Fellow feeling with the psychological pain (or pleasures) of a particular individual.

Particular sympathy: Fellow feeling with the pain (or pleasures) of a particular individual.

Utility: In her standard use, Grouchy uses "utility" to refer to common (or shared) or general interest. Sometimes it just means "usefulness."

FURTHER READINGS

Works by Sophie de Grouchy

Lettres sur la Sympathie suivies des Lettres d'Amour à Maillat Garat, edited by Jean-Paul Lagrave. Montreal: Presses de l'Universite du Quebec, 1993. An annotated edition of the French text, and also contains private letters written by Grouchy.

Les Lettres sur la Sympathies (1798) de Sophie de Grouchy: Philosophie morale et reforme sociale, edited by Marc-André Bernier and Deidre Dawson. Oxford: Voltaire Foundation, 2010. A scholarly edition of the French text, and contains articles discussing the text (in French).

Letters on Sympathy (1798): A Critical Edition," edited by Karin Brown, translated by James McClellan III. Transactions of the American Philosophical Society, New Series 98. Philadelphia, PA: American Philosophical Society, 2008. First English translation of the text.

Aux Origines de la République 1789-1792. Volume III: *Le Républicain par Condorcet et Thomas Paine, 1791,* by Nicolas de Condorcet and Thomas Paine. Paris: EDHIS, 1991. The integral copy of the four issues of *Le Républicain,* and contains two articles attributed to Grouchy.

"Achille du Chastellet et le Premier Mouvement Républicain en France d'Après des Lettres Inédites (1791-1792)," by Jean Martin. In *La Révolution Française, Revue Historique,* Nouvelle série 33. Paris: L. Maretheux, Imprimeur de la Cour d'Appel, 1927. Contains letters from Grouchy to Dumont, in which she talks about *Le Républicain,* and about her *Letters on Sympathy* and other writings.

Published Works Discussing Sophie de Grouchy

Bergès, Sandrine. "Is Motherhood Compatible with Political Participation? Sophie de Grouchy's Care-Based Republicanism." *Ethical Theory and Moral Practice* 18, no. 1 (2015): 47–60. A discussion of Grouchy on the centrality of the infant/carer relationship in the political growth of a nation.

Bergès, Sandrine. "Family, Gender, and Progress: Sophie de Grouchy and Her Exclusion in the Publication of Condorcet's *Sketch of Human Progress*." *Journal of the History of Ideas* 79, no.2 (April 2018): 267–283. A discussion of Grouchy's role in the writing and publication of Condorcet's *Sketch of Human Progress*.

Bréban, Laurie, and Jean Dellemotte. "From One Sympathy to Another: Sophie de Grouchy's Translation of and Commentary on Adam Smith's Theory of Moral Sentiments." *History of Political Economy* 49, no. 4 (2017): 667–707. An analysis of Grouchy's translation and *Letters* with special attention given to Grouchy's deviations from Smith's philosophy.

Dawson, Deirdre. "Is Sympathy So Surprising? Adam Smith and French Fictions of Sympathy." *Eighteenth-Century Scotland, Eighteenth-Century Life* 15, nos. 1 & 2 (1991): 147–162. A discussion of Grouchy's take on Smith's account of sympathy.

Dumont, Etienne. *Souvenirs sur Mirabeau et sur les deux premieres Assemblées Législatives.* Paris: Librairie de Charles Gosselin, 1832. Contains accounts of Dumont's interactions with Grouchy, and of the birth and demise of *Le Republicain*.

Forget, Evelyn L. "Cultivating Sympathy: Sophie Condorcet's Letters on Sympathy." *Journal of the History of Economic Thought* 23, no. 3 (2001): 319–337. A major introduction to Grouchy's thought and context and how Smith's views were taken to have political significance.

Guillois, Antoine. *La Marquise de Condorcet, Sa Famille, Son Salon, Ses Amis 1764–1822.* Paris: Paul Ollendorff, 1897. A biography commissioned by Grouchy's grandson.

Schliesser, Eric, ed. *Sympathy: A History.* Oxford: Oxford University Press, 2015. An edited volume that provides a philosophical history of reflection on sympathy, including Grouchy.

Schliesser, Eric. *Adam Smith: Systematic Philosopher and Public Thinker.* Oxford: Oxford University Press, 2017. Uses Grouchy to offer a systematic interpretation of Smith.

Schliesser, Eric. "Sophie de Grouchy: The Tradition(s) of Two Liberties, and the Missing Mother(s) of Liberalism." In *Women and Liberty: 1600–1800,* edited by J. Broad and K. Detlefsen, 109–122. Oxford: Oxford University Press, 2018. An attempt to re-insert Grouchy into the history of liberal reflection on two concepts of liberty.

Tegos, Spiros. "Sympathie morale et tragédie sociale: Sophie Grouchy lectrice d'Adam Smith." *Noesis* 21 (2013): 265–292. A scholarly article on Grouchy's reading of Smith.

Tegos, Spiros. "Friendship in Commercial Society Revisited." In *Propriety and Prosperity: New Studies on the Philosophy of Adam Smith,* edited by D. Hardwick and L. Marsh, 37–53. London: Palgrave Macmillan, 2014. Reads Grouchy as a republican and sentimentalist thinker in context.

Philosophical and Historical Background

Badinter, Elisabeth, and Robert Badinter. *Condorcet (1743–1794): Un Intellectuel en Politique.* Paris: Fayard, 1988. A biography of Condorcet in French. Elisabeth Badinter also has a short biographical notice of Grouchy in the Bernier and Dawson edition of the *Letters.*

Bergès, Sandrine, and Alan Coffee. *The Social and Political Philosophy of Mary Wollstonecraft.* Oxford: Oxford University Press, 2016. Chapters 7–11 in particular focus on Wollstonecraft's republicanism.

Schandeler, Jean-Pierre, and Pierre Crépel, eds. *Notes sur le Tableau Historique des progrès de l'esprit humain, projets, Esquisse, Fragments et Notes (1772–1794).* Paris: Institut National D'Etudes Démographiques, 2004. Transcription of all the documents relating to Condorcet's *Sketch* contained in the Institut library, and a detailed study of the differences between the various editions and the manuscript.

Whatmore, Richard. "Adam Smith's role in the French Revolution." *Past & present* 175 (2002): 65–89. Discusses Smith's reception in the French revolution, including by Condorcet and Grouchy.

Wolfe, Charles T. "Sensibility as vital force or as property of matter in mid-eighteenth-century debates." In *The Discourse of Sensibility,* edited by H.M. Lloyd, 147–170. Dordretch: Springer, 2013. Authoritative survey of the way sensibility was conceived in medical and philosophical circles in the eighteenth century.

Influences and Contemporaries

Cabanis, Pierre-Jean-George. *Rapports du Physique et du Moral de l'Homme* (1802). Paris: Hachette, 2017. Cabanis's treatise on physiology, written after years of research and dialogue with Sophie de Grouchy.

Condorcet, Nicolas. *Condorcet: Political Writings.* Edited by S. Lukes and Nadia Urbinani. Cambridge Texts in the History of Political Thought.

Cambridge: Cambridge University Press, 2012. Contains the *Sketch* (but not Grouchy's edition), his *Rights of Women to Citizenship*, and the *Advice* to his daughter in which he mentions his wife's other writings.

Fénelon, François de Salignac. *The Adventures of Telemachus*. Cambridge: Cambridge University Press, 1994. A very influential volume in France that led many to criticise the commercial society and to prefer a rural form of republicanism.

Locke, John. *An Essay Concerning Human Understanding*. Hammondsworth: Penguin Classics, 1998. Possibly one of the most influential texts in the philosophy of mind at the time Grouchy was writing. There are several direct and indirect references to it in the *Letters*.

Marcus Aurelius. *Meditations*. Hammondsworth: Penguin Classics, 1964. Young Sophie de Grouchy's bedtime reading.

Montesquieu, Charles, Baron. *The Spirit of the Laws*. Cambridge: Cambridge University Press, 1989. A treatise on laws and institutions with a strong republican flavor and many feminist aspects.

Paine, Thomas. *The Political Writings of Thomas Paine*. New York: Solomon King, 1830. Contains the original English version of Paine's advertisement for *Le Républicain*.

Rousseau, Jean-Jacques. *The Discourses and Other Early Political Writings*. Cambridge: Cambridge University Press, 1997. Probably the most influential works in political philosophy for revolutionary writers, including Grouchy.

Smith, Adam. *The Theory of Moral Sentiments*. In The Glasgow Edition of the Works and Correspondence of Adam Smith, edited by A. L. Macfie and D. D. Raphael. Indianapolis, IN: Liberty Fund, 1984. The text Grouchy is responding to in the *Letters* and translated for publication.

Tasso, Torquato. *The Liberation of Jerusalem*. Oxford: Oxford University Press. 2009. Grouchy translated this at convent school.

Wollstonecraft, Mary. *A Vindication of the Rights of Men, A Vindication of the Rights of Woman*. Edited by Janet Todd. Oxford: Oxford University Press, 1992. There are many interesting parallels between Wollstonecraft's and Grouchy's views on the role of education in a republic.

Young, Arthur. *A Tour in Ireland 1776–1779*. n.l: Book Jungle, 2008. Grouchy may have translated extracts from this book while at convent school.

BIBLIOGRAPHY

Primary Sources

Aristotle. *On Rhetoric.* Translated by George A. Kennedy. Oxford: Oxford University Press, 2006.

Beccaria, Cesare. *On Crimes and Punishments.* Translated by Graeme R. Newman and Pietro Marongiu, 5th ed. New Brunswick, NJ: Transaction, 2009.

Bernier, Marc-André, and Deidre Dawson, eds. *Les Lettres sur la Sympathies (1798) de Sophie de Grouchy: Philosophie morale et réforme sociale.* Oxford: Voltaire Foundation, 2010.

Brown, Karin, ed., and James McClellan III, trans. *Letters on Sympathy (1798): A Critical Edition.* Transactions of the American Philosophical Society, New Series 98. Philadephia, PA: American Philosophical Society, 2008.

Cabanis, Pierre-Jean-George. *Rapports du Physique et du Moral de l'Homme (1802).* Paris: Hachette, 2017.

Condorcet, Nicolas de. "Sur l'Admission des Femmes au droits de la cite." *Journal of the Society of 1789,* July 3, 1790.

Condorcet, Nicolas de. "Eloge d'Hunter." In *Oeuvres Complètes de Condorcet,* edited by Sophie de Grouchy, Pierre George Cabanis, and Dominique Joseph Garat. Paris and Brunswick: Henrichs, Fuchs, 1804.

Condorcet, Nicolas de. "On the Emancipation of Women." In *Condorcet: Political Writings,* edited by S. Lukes and N. Urbinati, 156–162. Cambridge: Cambridge University Press, 2012.

Condorcet, Nicolas de, and Thomas Paine. *Aux Origines de la République 1789–1792.* Volume 3: *Le Républicain par Condorcet et Thomas Paine, 1791.* Paris: EDHIS, 1991.

Dauban, Charles Aimé. *Etude sur Madame Roland et son temps*. Paris: Plon, 1864.

Dumont, Etienne. *Souvenirs sur Mirabeau et sur les deux premières Assemblées Législatives*. Paris: Librairie de Charles Gosselin, 1832.

Fénelon, François de Salignac. *The Adventures of Telemachus*. Edited by Patrick Riley. Cambridge: Cambridge University Press, 1994.

Gouges, Olympe de. *Femme réveille-toi! Déclaration des droits de la femme et de la citoyenne et autres ecrits*. Edited by Martine Reid. Paris: Gallimard, 2014.

Grouchy, Sophie de. *Théorie des Sentiments Moraux, suivi d'une Dissertation sur l'Origine des Langues, par Adam Smith, traduit de l'Anglais sur la septième et dernière édition, par S. Grouchy, Ve Condorcet. Elle y a joint huit Lettres sur la Sympathie*. Tome II. Paris: Buisson, 1798.

Grouchy, Sophie de. *Lettres sur la Sympathie suivies des Lettres d'Amour à Maillat Garat*. Edited by Jean-Paul Lagrave. Montreal: Presses de l'Université du Québec, 1993.

Hume, David. *Essays Moral, Political, and Literary*. Edited and with a foreword, notes, and glossary by Eugene F. Miller, with an appendix of variant readings from the 1889 edition by T. H. Green and T. H. Grose. Rev. ed. Indianapolis, IN: Liberty Fund, 1987.

Kant, Immanuel. *Anthropology from a Pragmatic Point of View*. Translated by Victor Lyle Dowdell. Carbondale and Edwardsville: Southern Illinois University Press, 1996.

Locke, John. *An Essay Concerning Human Understanding*. Hammondsworth: Penguin Classics, 1998.

Lukes, Steven, and Nadia Urbinani, eds. *Condorcet: Political Writings*. Cambridge: Cambridge University Press, 2012.

Marcus Aurelius. *Meditations*. Hammondsworth: Penguin Classics, 1964.

Mill, John Stuart. *On Liberty and Other Essays*. Edited by John Gray. Oxford World Classics. Oxford: Oxford University Press, 1998.

Montesquieu, Charles. *The Spirit of the Laws*. Edited by Anne M. Cohler, Basia C. Miller, and Harold S. Stone. Cambridge: Cambridge University Press, 1989.

Paine, Thomas. *The Political Writings of Thomas Paine*, vol. 1. New York: Solomon King, 1830.

Roland, Marie-Jeanne Phlipon. *Lettres de Madame Roland (1780–1793)*, vol. 2. Edited by Claude Perroud. Paris: Imprimerie Nationale, 1900.

Rousseau, Jean-Jacques. *The Discourses and Other Early Political Writings*. Cambridge: Cambridge University Press, 1997.

Rousseau, Jean-Jacques. *Emile: Or on Education*. Translated by Barbara Foxley. London: Everyman Classics, 1991.

Seneca. *Epistles*. Translated by Richard Gunmere. Loeb Classical Library, vol. 10. Cambridge, MA: Harvard University Press, 1917.

Smith, Adam. *An Inquiry into the Nature and Causes of the Wealth of Nations*. In *The Glasgow Edition of the Works and Correspondence of Adam Smith*, edited by R.

H. Campbell, A. S. Skinner, and W. B. Todd, vol. 2. Indianapolis, IN: Liberty Fund, 1981.

Smith, Adam. *The Theory of Moral Sentiments*. In The Glasgow Edition of the Works and Correspondence of Adam Smith, edited by A. L. Macfie and D. D. Raphael. Vol 1. Indianapolis, IN: Liberty Fund, 1984.

Tasso, Torquato. *The Liberation of Jerusalem*. Oxford: Oxford University Press, 2009.

Turgot, Anne-Robert-Jacques. *Reflections on the Formation and the Distribution of Riches*. Translated by William J. Ashley. New York: Macmillan, 1898.

Voltaire, *Oeuvres Complètes*. Edited by Jean Michel Moreau, marquis de Jean-Antoine-Nicolas de Caritat Condorcet, Louis Moland, Georges Bengesco, Adrien Jean Quentin Beuchot, vol. 52. Paris: Garniers Freres, 1877–1885.

Voltaire, *The Works of Voltaire: A Contemporary Version*, edited by John Morley, trans. William F. Fleming New York: E.R. DuMont, 1901

Wollstonecraft, Mary. *Thoughts on the Education of Daughters*. London: J. Johnson, 1787.

Wollstonecraft, Mary. *A Vindication of the Rights of Men, A Vindication of the Rights of Woman*. Edited by Janet Todd. Oxford: Oxford University Press, 1992.

Young, Arthur. *A Tour in Ireland 1776–1779*. n.l: Book Jungle, 2008.

Secondary Sources

Badinter, Elisabeth, and Robert Badinter. *Condorcet: Un Intellectual en Politique*. Paris: Fayard, 1988.

Bergès, Sandrine. *A Feminist Perspective on Virtue Ethics*. London: Palgrave Macmillan, 2014.

Bergès, Sandrine. "Wet-Nursing and Political Participation: The Republican Approaches to Motherhood in Mary Wollstonecraft and Sophie de Grouchy." In *The Social and Political Philosophy of Mary Wollstonecraft*, edited by Sandrine Bergès and Alan Coffee, 201–217. Oxford: Oxford University Press, 2016.

Bergès, Sandrine. "Family, Gender, and Progress: Sophie de Grouchy and Her Exclusion in the Publication of Condorcet's *Sketch of Human Progress*." *Journal of the History of Ideas* 79, no. 2 (2018): 267–283.

Bergès, Sandrine, and Alan Coffee. *The Social and Political Philosophy of Mary Wollstonecraft*. Oxford: Oxford University Press, 2016.

Carrasco, María Alejandra. "Adam Smith's Reconstruction of Practical Reason." *Review of Metaphysics* 58, no. 1 (2004): 81–116.

Carroll, Noel. "The Nature of Horror." *Journal of Aesthetics and Art Criticism* 46, no. 1 (1987): 51–59.

Deslauriers, Marguerite. "Marinella and Her Interlocutors, Hot Blood, Hot Words, Hot Deeds." *Philosophical Studies* 174, no. 10 (2017): 2525–2537.

Faccarello, Gilbert, and Philippe Steiner. "The Diffusion of the Work of Adam Smith in the French Language: An Outline History." In *A Critical Bibliography of Adam Smith*, edited by Keith Tribe, 61–119. London: Pickering and Chatto, 2002.

Gill, Michael B. "Moral Pluralism in Smith and His Contemporaries." *Revue internationale de philosophie* 3 (2014): 275–306.

Groenewegen, Peter. "Turgot and Adam Smith." *Scottish Journal of Political Economy* 16, no. 3 (1969): 271–287.

Guillois, Antoine. *La Marquise de Condorcet, Sa Famille, Son Salon, Ses Amis 1764–1822*. Paris: Paul Ollendorff, 1897.

Halldenius, Lena. *Mary Wollstonecraft and Feminist Republicanism*. London: Routledge, 2015.

Hanley, Ryan Patrick. "Commerce and Corruption: Rousseau's Diagnosis and Adam Smith's Cure." *European Journal of Political Theory* 7, no. 2 (2008): 137–158.

Hanley, Ryan Patrick. "David Hume and the "Politics of Humanity." *Political Theory* 39, no. 2 (2011): 205–233.

Hanley, Ryan Patrick. "Adam Smith and Virtue." In *Oxford Handbook of Adam Smith*, edited by C. Berry, C. Smith, and M. P. Paganelli, 230–232. Oxford: Oxford University Press, 2013.

Hanley, Ryan Patrick. "Fénelon's *Telemachus*." In *Ten Neglected Classics of Philosophy*, edited by Eric Schliesser, 26–54. Oxford: Oxford University Press, 2016.

Haraszti, Zoltán. "John Adams Flays a Philosophe: Annotations on Condorcet's Progress of the Human Mind." *William and Mary Quarterly* 7, no. 2 (1950): 223–254.

Herzog, Lisa. "Adam Smith on markets and justice." *Philosophy Compass* 9, no. 12 (2014): 864–875.

Hesse, Carla. *The Other Enlightenment: How French Women Became Modern*. Princeton, NJ: Princeton University Press, 2001.

Hont, István. "The Early Enlightenment Debate on Commerce and Luxury." In *Cambridge History of Eighteenth-Century Political Thought*, edited by Mark Goldie and Robert Wokler, 379–418. Cambridge: Cambridge University Press, 2006.

Lainey, Yves. "Vauvenargues and His Work." *Theoria: A Journal of Social and Political Theory* 27 (1966): 21–30.

Martin, Jean. "Achille du Chastellet et le Premier Mouvement Républicain en France d'Après des Lettres Inédites (1791–1792)." In *La Révolution Française, Revue Historique*, Nouvelle série 33, 104–132. Paris: L. Maretheux, Imprimeur de la Cour d'Appel, 1927.

McLean, Ian, and Fiona Hewitt, eds. *Condorcet: Foundations of Social Choice and Political Theory*. Cheltenham: Edward Elgar, 1994.

McMurran, Mary Helen. *The Spread of Novels: Translation and Prose Fiction in the Eighteenth Century*. Princeton, NJ: Princeton University Press, 2009.

O'Neill, Eileen "Disappearing Ink: Early Modern Women Philosophers and Their Fate in History." In *Philosophy in a Feminist Voice: Critiques and Reconstructions*, edited by Janet A. Kourany, 17–62. Princeton, NJ: Princeton University Press, 1998.

Percival, Melissa. *The Appearance of Character: Physiognomy and Facial Expression in Eighteenth-Century France*, vol. 47. Cambridge: MHRA, 1999.

Pisanelli. Simona. "Adam Smith and the Marquis de Condorcet. Did They Really Meet?" *Iberian Journal for the History of Economic Thought* 2 (2015): 21–35.

Riskin, Jessica. *Science in the Age of Sensibility: The Sentimental Empiricists of the French Enlightenment*. Chicago: University of Chicago Press, 2002.

Salter, John. "Grotius and Pufendorf on the Right of Necessity." *History of Political Thought* 26, no. 2 (2005): 285–302.

Schandeler, Jean-Pierre, and Pierre Crépel, eds. *Notes sur le Tableau Historique des progrès de l'esprit humain, projets, Esquisse, Fragments et Notes (1772–1794)*. Paris: Institut National D'Etudes Démographiques. 2004.

Schliesser, Eric. "Reading Adam Smith after Darwin: On the Evolution of Propensities, Institutions, and Sentiments." *Journal of Economic Behavior & Organization* 77, no. 1 (2011): 14–22.

Schliesser, Eric. "Counterfactual Causal Reasoning in Smithian Sympathy." *Revue internationale de philosophie* 3 (2014): 307–316.

Schliesser, Eric, ed. *Sympathy: A History*. Oxford: Oxford University Press, 2015.

Schliesser, Eric. *Adam Smith: Systematic Philosopher and Public Thinker*. Oxford: Oxford University Press, 2017.

Schliesser, Eric. "Sophie de Grouchy: The Tradition(s) of Two Liberties, and the Missing Mother(s) of Liberalism." In *Women and Liberty, 1600–1800: Philosophical Essays*, edited by Jacqueline Broad and Karen Detlefsen, 109–122. Oxford: Oxford University Press, 2017.

Schliesser, Eric. "On Philosophical Translator-Advocates and Linguistic Injustice." *Philosophical Papers* 47, no. 1 (2018): 93-121.

Schliesser, Eric. "Sophie de Grouchy, Marquise de Condorcet: wisdom and reform between reason and feeling." In *Feminist History of Philosophy: The Recovery and Evaluation of Women's Philosophical Thought*, edited by Eileen O'Neill and Marcy P. Lascano. Dordrecht Springer,Forthcoming.

Taylor, Jacqueline. "Hume on the Importance of Humanity," *Revue internationale de philosophie* 1 (2013): 81–97.

Tegos, Spiros. "Sympathie moral et tragédie sociale: Sophie Grouchy lectrice d'Adam Smith." *Noesis* 21 (2013): 265–292.

Tegos, Spiros. "Friendship in Commercial Society Revisited." In *Propriety and Prosperity: New Studies on the Philosophy of Adam Smith*, edited by D. Hardwick and L. Marsh, 37–53. London: Palgrave Macmillan, 2014.

Wasserman, Earl R. "The Pleasures of Tragedy." *ELH* 14, no. 4 (1947): 283–307.

Wolfe, Charles T. "Sensibility as Vital Force or as Property of Matter in Mid-Eighteenth-Century Debates." In *The Discourse of Sensibility*, edited by H. M. Lloyd, 147–170. Dordrecht: Springer, 2013.

INDEX

Printed in the USA/Agawam, MA
January 6, 2021

767861.002